Green Building and LEED Core Concepts Guide

Purchase agreement and license to use GREEN BUILDING AND LEED CORE CONCEPTS GUIDE

CONTENTS

INTRODUCTION

Green building is an integrative effort to transform the way built environments—from individual buildings to neighborhoods and even entire communities—are designed, constructed, and operated. The scope of green building reaches from the earliest stages of planning to beyond the end of a structure's life. It runs up and down the supply chain. It encompasses the production and fate of every substance that goes into or out of a project. The sweeping scope of green building requires a cross-cutting, interdisciplinary approach.

This guide presents green building concepts and strategies and introduces the ideas and practices that serve as the foundation for more detailed study of green building, particularly as it relates to the green building rating systems of the Leadership in Energy and Environmental Design (LEED) program and to individual market segments, such as homes, commercial new construction, and neighborhood developments.

We first describe how green building aspires to transform the design, construction, and operation of built environments and shift practice toward higher performance, lower environmental impact, and ultimately regenerative designs. The section that follows describes the certification approach used by the U.S. Green Building Council and its LEED rating systems. LEED is not an end in itself but a tool that helps create high-performance, more sustainable built environments by providing a framework for design, construction, and evaluation. It is up to green building professionals to use this tool as part of an integrated planning and design process to achieve real results on the ground.

Green building requires a holistic, integrated approach but in practice depends on new strategies in the various aspects of design and construction. Accordingly, the heart of this book is an introduction to the six categories used in LEED:

- Sustainable Sites
- Water Efficiency
- Energy and Atmosphere
- Materials and Resources
- Indoor Environmental Quality
- Innovation in Design

Each chapter reviews the basic concepts and strategies associated with each credit category, while recognizing that they are all intimately linked and must be considered together during effective integrative processes.

> Throughout, the reader will find references to sources of information for green building professionals. We also offer examples of challenging questions facing the green building community—many of which lack straightforward answers—to encourage more detailed study based on real-world projects.

At the end, a glossary defines terms that may be unfamiliar to some readers or have specific meanings in the context of green building.

Having absorbed the basics of green building concepts and strategies, the reader can move forward on more specialized pathways. Depending on one's field in the building industry, a logical next step might be to study the relevant LEED reference guide:

- *LEED Reference Guide for Green Building Design and Construction,* which covers the New Construction, Core & Shell, Schools, Healthcare, and Retail rating systems;
- *LEED Reference Guide for Green Building Interior Design and Construction,* which covers the Commercial Interiors and Retail Interiors rating systems;
- *LEED Reference Guide for Green Building Operations and Maintenance,* which covers the Existing Buildings and Existing Schools rating systems; or
- *LEED for Homes Reference Guide,* which covers the Homes rating system.

Specialized educational programs also offer detailed understanding for the rating systems. Readers interested in more in-depth technical training may wish to focus on specific elements, such as energy modeling or lighting design. More information about educational opportunities in all of these areas is available at www.usgbc.org.

GREEN BUILDING

The green building movement strives to create a permanent shift in prevailing design, planning, construction, and operational practices toward lower-impact, more sustainable, and ultimately regenerative built environments. This transformation will never be complete, since green building is fundamentally a process of continual improvement. In this process, today's "best practices" become tomorrow's standard practices and the foundation for ever-higher levels of performance.

Why is green building necessary?

The answer is rooted in the effects of conventional buildings and land use on people, the environment, and our shared natural resources. The cumulative impact of the design, construction, and operation of built environments has profound implications for human health, the environment, and the economy. For example, with conventional development practices,

- Clearing of land for development often destroys wildlife habitat;
- Extracting, manufacturing, and transporting materials contribute to the pollution of water and air, the release of toxic chemicals, and the emission of greenhouse gases;
- Building operations require large inputs of energy and water and generate substantial waste streams; and
- Building-related transportation, such as commuting and services, contributes to a wide range of impacts associated with vehicle use, energy consumption, and harmful environmental effects.

In the United States, buildings account for a high proportion of resource use and waste generation:

- 14% of potable water consumption;
- 30% of waste output;
- 38% of carbon dioxide emissions;
- 40% of raw materials use;
- 24% to 50% of energy use; and
- 72% of electricity consumption.[1]

Modifying the conventional way in which homes, schools, offices, shopping centers, hospitals, and cities are designed can have a beneficial effect on the environment. Green building practices can minimize human use of natural resources while generating economic benefits that include lower operational costs and higher human productivity. Green buildings are efficient and comfortable, and they contain the amenities needed for a better quality of life, including improved health.

> Many of the elements of green building are not new or even unique. For example, energy efficiency, Smart Growth, water conservation, and indoor air quality have been the focus of various programs and incentives, both governmental and market driven. What distinguishes green building is its focus on *all* of these issues in an effort to contribute solutions to pressing health, environmental, and economic challenges through the location, design, construction, and operation of buildings.

The trend in the United States toward green building practices has quickened in the past decade, contributing to a market transformation in the supply of building products, and services—and in the demand for skilled professionals. The value of green building construction is projected to increase to $60 billion by 2010.[2] The facts are staggering. The Green Building Alliance anticipates that the market for green building products will be worth $30 billion to $40 billion annually by 2010.[3] As more green products and technologies become available, the more mainstream green building becomes.

Federal, state, and local governments have all adopted more sustainable building practices. For example, the U.S. General Services Administration requires that all new federal government construction projects and substantial renovations achieve LEED certification, and it encourages projects to achieve at least a Silver rating. Government agencies, utility companies, and manufacturers increasingly offer financial incentives for developers and owners to enhance the environmental performance of their buildings.

1 Energy Information Administration. 2005. EIA Annual Energy Review and Energy Information Administration. Emissions of Greenhouse Gases in the United States.

2 McGraw-Hill Construction. 2008. Key Trends in the European and U.S. Construction Marketplace: SmartMarket Report.

3 Green Building Alliance. 2006. USGBC Green Building Facts. http://www.usgbc.org/ShowFile.aspx?DocumentID=3340.

THINK ABOUT IT

The future of the built environment. Conventional building practices are not sustainable. They use too much energy, create too much waste, and sometimes even undermine the health and comfort of occupants. Conventional patterns of energy use, waste, and pollution do not support widely accepted goals for greenhouse gas emissions reductions and public health. Recognizing the problem, however, is only the first step toward a solution. What might the built environment of 2030 look like? How can we break from the status quo and achieve results at scale?

Primary Resources: Energy Usage in Buildings

Buildings are exceptionally costly investments. Their owners must have access to large amounts of capital and sufficient revenue to meet operations and maintenance costs. The design, construction, and operation of buildings also have social, economic, and environmental consequences for occupants and society.

Since 1979, the U.S. Department of Energy's Energy Information Administration (EIA) has collected data on both commercial and residential buildings through its energy consumption surveys, which provide periodic national assessments.

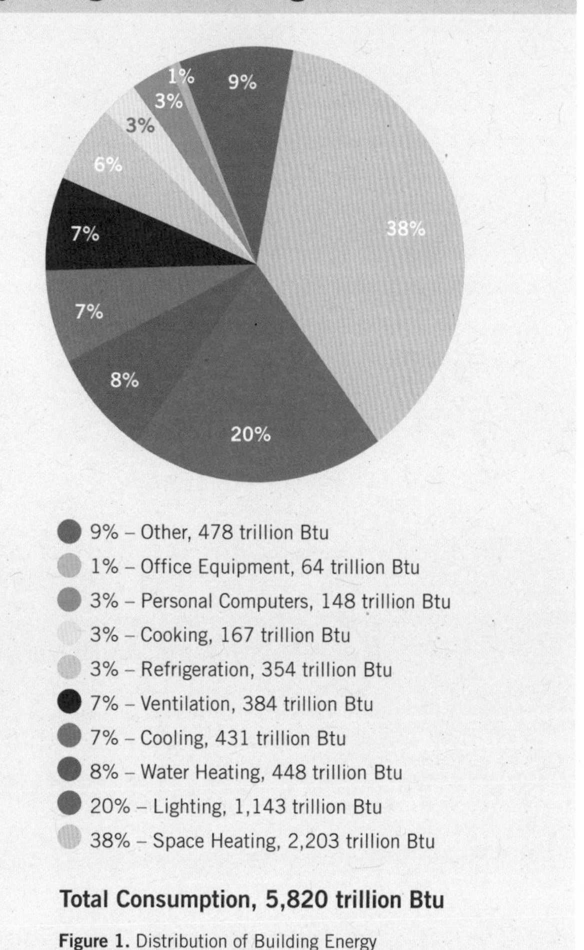

Figure 1. Distribution of Building Energy Use (Source: U.S. DOE, Energy Information Administration)

According to a recent Commercial Building Energy Consumption Survey, in 2003 the United States had 4.9 million commercial buildings with 71.6 billion square feet of floor space. These buildings used 6,500 trillion Btus of energy, of which electricity accounted for 55% and natural gas, 32%. Of this energy, 36% was used for space heating and 21% for lighting. In 2003, owners and operators of commercial buildings spent $92 billion on energy, not including transportation-related energy costs. For an average 13,000-square-foot building, this amounted to nearly $20,000 per year, or $1.43 per square foot.

EIA's 2005 Residential Energy Consumption Survey collected data from 4,381 households that statistically represented the 111.1 million housing units in the United States. The results indicated that U.S. households spent a total of $201 billion on energy in 2005, equivalent to $1,810 per household, or $0.83 per square foot.

A focus on green building and energy efficiency can dramatically reduce such costs for both commercial and residential owners, and the savings continue to grow throughout the lifetime of the building.

In 2001, the EIA estimated that Americans drove 2,287 billion vehicle miles, consuming 113 billion gallons of gasoline and spending $150.3 billion on fuel. The combustion of all that fuel released 837 million metric tons of carbon dioxide (CO_2) into the atmosphere. Our dependence on cars affects local air quality, public safety, and quality of life—impacts that could be significantly reduced by smart location of buildings and better land-use planning.

- Energy Information Administration, end-use energy consumption data and analyses. http://www.eia.doe.gov/emeu/consumption/index.html.
- 2003 Commercial Building Energy Consumption Survey. http://www.eia.doe.gov/emeu/cbecs/cbecs2003/detailed_tables_2003/detailed_tables_2003.html#consumexpen03.
- 2005 Residential Energy Consumption Survey. http://www.eia.doe.gov/emeu/recs/recs2005/c&e/detailed_tables2005c&e.html.

LIFE CYCLE OF BUILT ENVIRONMENTS

Sustainability is not a singular event; it has no crisp beginning or end. Rather, it is a process of continual improvement. When applied to built environments, sustainability begins at the inception of an idea and continues seamlessly until the project reaches the end of its life and its parts are recycled or reused. The study of this continual process, known as life-cycle assessment, encompasses planning, design, construction, operations, and ultimately retirement and renewal. The analysis considers not only the building itself but also its materials and components, from their extraction, manufacture, and transport to their use, reuse, recycling, and disposal. The intent of life-cycle assessment is to inform the choice of building materials and systems and thereby minimize the negative impacts of buildings and land use on people and the environment. Moreover, as sustainable design and operations improve, we aspire to create environments that truly regenerate their surroundings, creating positive impacts.

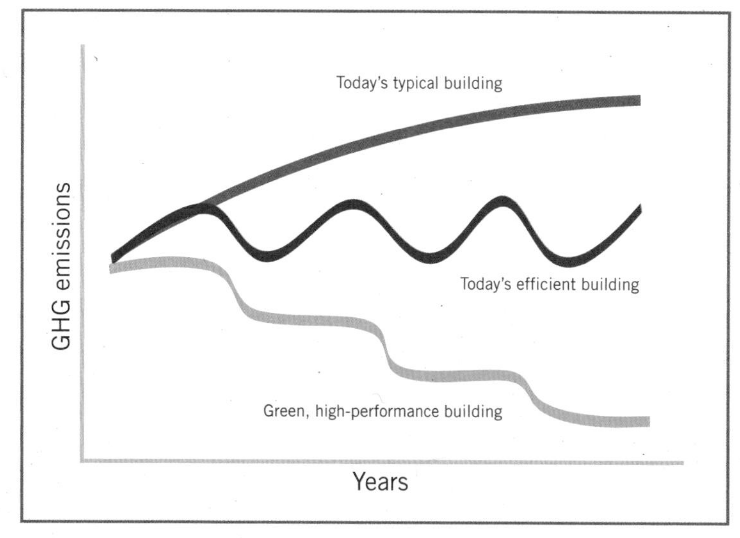

Figure 2. GHG Emissions over Lifecycle of Different Buildings (Source: CTG Energetics, Inc. 2009)

Sustainable design requires consideration of the entire life of a building. This perspective contrasts with the conventional narrow focus on capital or construction costs, and it allows for a balance between initial costs (or first costs, or capital costs) and costs incurred during operations and at the end of life. Life-cycle cost analyses permit a comparison of different designs and identify the best long-term investment—the approach that offers the lowest overall cost of ownership consistent with the project goals and available resources. All the building expenses that can be calculated are included in the analysis: initial costs (design and construction), operating costs (energy, water, other utilities, and personnel), and maintenance, repair, and replacement costs. Life-cycle cost analysis identifies which high-performance building systems will save money over the life of a project, despite their higher initial cost, and thus it allows owners to invest in long-term performance.

INTEGRATIVE APPROACH

In many endeavors, disciplinary boundaries and linear planning and design processes can lead to inefficient solutions. The concept of an integrative approach has emerged as a new paradigm that emphasizes connections and communication among professionals throughout the life of a project. Bringing building owners, operators, architects, planners, engineers, and contractors together and working through an integrative process of observation and analysis allow building teams to cross traditional barriers and develop innovative solutions. The term integrative design is most often applied to a new construction design process; however, the concept of integrative design is applicable to any phase in the life cycle of a building or land-use project.

The building design process begins when the basic programmatic needs and requirements for the project are determined. Schematic design follows, as the basic scheme that will be used to meet the project goals is developed. During design development, the scheme is further refined into a design, and each component of that design is fleshed out. Finally, construction documents are prepared to translate the design into something that can then be built.

In a conventional design process, the architect, the engineers (civil, mechanical, electrical, plumbing, structural), the landscape architect, the construction contractors, and others all work relatively independently on their individual scopes of work, handing off work products to other professionals along the way. This separation of the disciplines and generally linear design process can limit opportunities for integration and synergy, particularly with construction contractors and other specialists who traditionally become engaged only toward the end of the process.

In contrast, in an integrative design process, all the disciplines come together at the beginning to discuss the project goals and requirements. A clear statement of sustainability and performance goals guides this team to find new approaches to the project. As the project progresses through the design phases, each element of the design is reviewed to verify that it meets the original goals and intent of the owner. In this way, the project team engages in a more integrative approach that allows for deeper integration and collaborative problem solving.

In an integrative process, the property owner, facility managers, designers, construction contractors, and other project team members establish a mutual understanding of the project's goals, priorities, and budget as early as possible. Input from the major stakeholders and members of the design team is essential before schematic design begins, particularly since many of the decisions associated with environmental impacts are made early in the design process, starting with the location of the project. Site selection can have substantial long-term impacts on building performance and determine how the building affects the natural environment, as these examples indicate:

- Walkable access to public transit or shops and services can reduce transportation-related energy and associated environmental impacts.
- Building orientation can increase the availability of natural daylight, which can be used to reduce demand for artificial lighting and the need for mechanical heating and cooling.
- Building and site design and orientation can change the amount and quality of open space and management of stormwater.

Integrative design also provides opportunities to approach resources in new ways. For example, in the conventional process, plumbing engineers, mechanical engineers, civil engineers, and landscape designers all consider water—potable water supply, wastewater disposal, stormwater runoff, irrigation demand—but make their plans separately. An integrative design process, in contrast, al-

Project Case Study

©Melissa Raddatz (Busby Perkins+Will)

Dockside Green

Dockside Green in Victoria, British Columbia, is one of the most innovative examples of integrative design in the world. A 15-acre mixed-use harbor community with commercial space and three residential neighborhoods, the facility is distinguished by its comprehensive attention to integrative design. The project team aggressively pursued synergies to achieve sustainability goals. The project has multiple "closed-loop" systems where the output from one process serves as the input to another: rainwater is captured for domestic use, for example, and domestic wastewater is then used for landscape irrigation. The project uses state-of-the-art strategies for onsite biomass heat generation, onsite stormwater and sewage treatment, strict water conservation measures, and provisions for alternative transportation. The result is an exceptionally energy-efficient facility with very low greenhouse gas emissions. These features helped the Dockside Green community achieve a LEED Platinum certification while creating new jobs, supporting local suppliers, and providing educational opportunities.

For more information, visit http://docksidegreen.com/sustainability/overview/overview.html.

lows these professionals to think holistically about water as a resource. This kind of collaboration can lead to the design of systems that capture stormwater and graywater to meet water supply and irrigation needs while reducing runoff and protecting water quality.

The overall benefits of a sustainable building are maximized through an integrative approach. Strategic planning that focuses on sustainability, starting early in design and continuing through the project, can open up opportunities for better indoor air quality, reduced environmental impacts, improved occupant comfort, low or no increase in construction costs for sustainable elements, optimized return on investment, and reduced operations and maintenance costs.

Primary Resources: Integrative Design

The integrative approach requires a fundamental shift in the mindset of project teams. In many cases, team members must step out of their traditional silos and jump into often unfamiliar processes, such as systems thinking and nonhierarchical leadership.

- *Developing Sustainable Planned Communities* (Urban Land Institute, 2007).
- *Green Building through Integrated Design,* by Jerry Yudelson (McGraw-Hill GreenSource, 2008).
- *The Integrative Design Guide to Green Building,* by Becker Reed (John Wiley & Sons, 2009).
- *Sustainable Building Technical Manual: Green Building Design, Construction, and Operations* (U.S. Green Building Council, 1996). http://www.scribd.com/doc/7423187/Sustainable-Building-Technical-Manual.

GREEN BUILDING COSTS AND BENEFITS

On average, green buildings perform better than conventional ones. They save energy, use less water, generate less waste, and provide healthier, more comfortable indoor environments. A recent study by the New Buildings Institute found that in green buildings, average energy use intensities (energy consumed per unit of floor space) are 24% lower than in typical buildings. The U.S. General Services Administration surveyed 12 green buildings in its portfolio and found these savings and improvements:

- 13% lower maintenance costs;
- 26% less energy usage;
- 27% higher levels of occupant satisfaction; and
- 33% lower CO_2 emissions.[4]

4 General Services Administration, Public Buildings Service. 2008. Assessing Green Building Performance: A Post Occupancy Evaluation of 12 GSA Buildings.

The study concluded that the federal government's green buildings outperform national averages in all measured performance areas—energy, operating costs, water use, occupant satisfaction, and carbon emissions—and that buildings achieving LEED Gold certification achieve the best overall performance. The agency attributed this performance to a fully integrated approach to sustainable design that addressed environmental, financial, and occupant satisfaction issues.

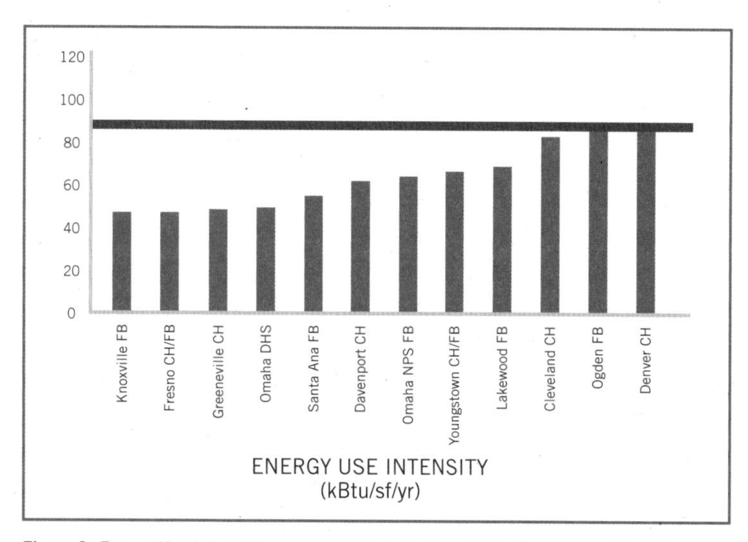

Figure 3. Energy Use Intensities for Sustainably Designed U.S. Government Buildings (Source: GSA 2008)
The red bar indicates the national average energy use intensity.

Making buildings more comfortable and productive for their occupants has special significance in light of studies conducted by the U.S. Environmental Protection Agency (EPA), which found that people in the United States spend, on average, 90% of their time indoors, where they may be exposed to pollutant concentrations two to 100 times higher than outdoor levels. Occupants of green buildings typically have significantly greater satisfaction with air quality and lighting than occupants of conventional buildings. Case studies show that these benefits can translate into a 2% to 16% increase in workers' and students' productivity. And even small increases in productivity dramatically increase the value of the building.

What is the cost of these benefits? If we view sustainability as an added feature of a building, we would consider efforts to reduce energy costs or improve indoor environmental quality comparable to specifying a better grade of countertop or a more impressive front door: any improvement beyond a minimally code-compliant baseline is an added cost. This perspective often leads to conclusions that green buildings cost slightly more than conventional buildings, with estimates ranging from 2% to more than 5%. If, however, we consider energy improvements as part of an integrative design, the added costs are often balanced by new savings. For instance, specification of more costly, high-performance windows may allow for the use of a smaller, lower-cost heating, ventilation, and air-conditioning (HVAC) system. More fundamentally, if we view sustainable design as part of the necessary functional requirements for building an energy-efficient structure and providing a safe, healthful indoor environment, we can compare the cost of the green building with that of other buildings in the same class rather than against an artificial baseline.

> A landmark study by the firm Davis Langdon found no significant difference between the average cost of a LEED-certified building and other new construction in the same category: there are expensive green buildings, and there are expensive conventional buildings. Certification as a green building was not a significant predictor of building cost.

Interestingly, the public dramatically overestimates the marginal cost of green building. A 2007 public opinion survey conducted by the World Business Council for Sustainable Development[5] found that respondents believed that green building features added 17% to the cost of a building, whereas a survey of 146 green buildings found an actual average marginal cost of less than 2%.

Yet green building is a significant predictor of tangible improvements in building performance, and those improvements have considerable value. Studies have shown that certified green buildings command significantly higher rents. A University of California–Berkeley study[6] analyzed 694 certified green buildings and compared them with 7,489 other office buildings, each located within a quarter-mile of a green building in the sample. The researchers found that, on average, certified green office buildings rent for 2% more than comparable nearby buildings. After adjusting for occupancy levels, they identified a 6% premium for certified buildings. The researchers calculated that at prevailing capitalization rates, this adds more than $5 million to the market value of each property.

Primary Resources: The cost of green

Statistically, green buildings cost no more than their conventional counterparts. Figure 1 illustrates findings for academic buildings. Total design and construction costs range between approximately $250 and $575 per square foot. Certified buildings have a wide range of costs, and they are statistically indistinguishable from conventional buildings.

- "Cost of Green Revisited: Reexamining the Feasibility and Cost Impact of Sustainable Design in the Light of Increased Market Adoption," by Lisa Fay Matthiessen and Peter Morris (Davis Langdon, 2007). http://www.davislangdon.com/USA/Research/ResearchFinder/2007-The-Cost-of-Green-Revisited/.

5 Green Buildings and Communities: Costs and Benefits, by Greg Kats et al. (Good Energies, 2008).

6 "Doing Well by Doing Good? Green Office Buildings," by Piet Eichholtz, Nils Kok, and John M. Quigley (Institute of Business and Economic Research, University of California–Berkeley, 2008). http://www.mistra.org/download/18.39aa239f11a8dd8de6b800026477/IBER+Green+Office+Buildings+NKok+et+al.pdf.

- "Costing Green: A Comprehensive Cost Database and Budgeting Methodology," by Lisa Fay Matthiessen and Peter Morris (Davis Langdon, 2004). http://www.usgbc.org/Docs/Resources/Cost_of_Green_Full.pdf.
- "Doing Well by Doing Good? Green Office Buildings," by Piet Eichholtz, Nils Kok, and John M. Quigley (Institute of Business and Economic Research, University of California–Berkeley, 2008). http://www.mistra.org/download/18.39aa239f11a8dd8de6b800026477/IBER+Green+Office+Buildings+NKok+et+al.pdf.
- *Greening Buildings and Communities: Costs and Benefits,* by Greg Kats et al. (Good Energies, 2008). http://www.goodenergies.com/news/research-knowledge.php?WYSESSID=j1lrode5oi105htjjcjtbi5ud1.

THINK ABOUT IT

The cost of green building. Does green building cost more, and does achieving higher levels of LEED certification add cost? Can LEED certification be achieved in ways that lower costs?

U.S. GREEN BUILDING COUNCIL AND ITS PROGRAMS

The U.S. Green Building Council (USGBC) is the nation's foremost coalition of leaders from every sector of the building industry working to promote buildings that are environmentally responsible, profitable, and healthful places to live and work. USGBC is a nonprofit organization whose members represent more than 15,000 organizations across the industry and include building owners and end users, real estate developers, facility managers, architects, designers, engineers, general contractors, subcontractors, product and building system manufacturers, government agencies, and nonprofits. USGBC provides educational opportunities to learn more about sustainable design strategies. Green building professionals can join one of the more than 70 regional USGBC chapters across the country that provide green building resources, education, and networking opportunities.

USGBC'S MISSION

To transform the way buildings and communities are designed, built, and operated, enabling an environmentally and socially responsible, healthy, and prosperous environment that improves the quality of life.

LEADERSHIP IN ENERGY AND ENVIRONMENTAL DESIGN

The Leadership in Energy and Environmental Design™ (LEED) Rating System was created by USGBC to provide a framework for meeting sustainability goals and assessing building performance. Voluntary and consensus-based, LEED addresses all building types.

> LEED is a third-party green building certification program and the nationally accepted benchmark for the design, construction, and operation of high-performance green buildings and neighborhoods. LEED gives building owners and operators the tools they need to have an immediate and measurable impact on their buildings' performance. LEED promotes a whole-building approach to sustainability by recognizing performance in location and planning, sustainable site development, water savings, energy efficiency, materials selection, indoor environmental quality, innovative strategies, and attention to priority regional issues.

LEED measures and enhances the design and sustainability of buildings based on a "triple bottom line" approach. The term was coined by John Elkington in 1994 to refocus the measurement of corporate performance from the perspective of a shareholder (predominantly financially driven) to that of a stakeholder (anyone affected by the actions of a firm) and coordinate three interests: "people, planet, and profit." USGBC has adapted the triple bottom line to establish metrics and rating systems to measure and recognize building projects based on their performance in the three corresponding dimensions of sustainability: society, the environment, and the economy.

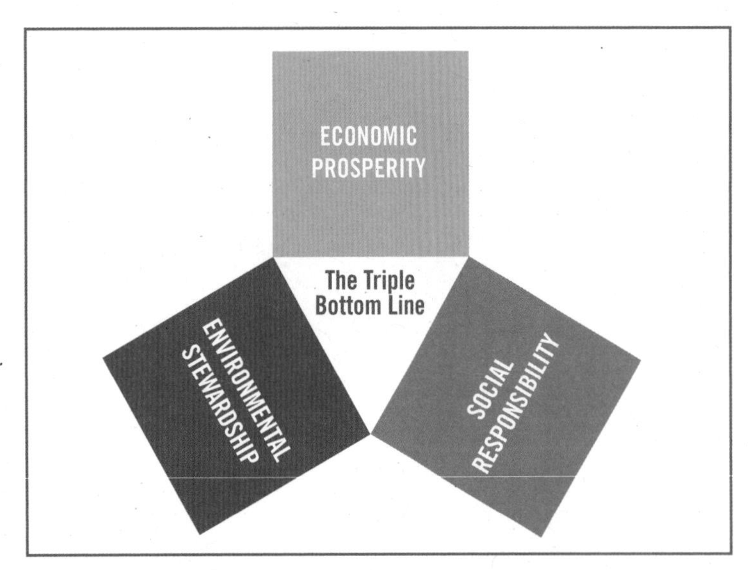

Figure 4. The Triple Bottom Line

The three dimensions are often likened to the three legs of a stool. If the legs are not all equal, the stool will wobble and be unable to perform its function. Projects certified under the LEED rating systems demonstrate, through compliance with a range of requirements, that they have addressed elements that balance and enhance all three areas of the triple bottom line, all three dimensions of sustainability.

GREEN BUILDING CERTIFICATION INSTITUTE

In 2007, the Green Building Certification Institute (GBCI) was established as a separately incorporated entity with the support of the U.S. Green Building Council. GBCI administers credentialing programs related to green building practice. USGBC handles the development of the LEED rating systems and offers LEED-based education and research programs; GBCI administers the LEED Professional Accreditation program independently, to allow for balanced, objective management of the credential.

GBCI manages all aspects of the LEED Professional Accreditation program, including exam development, registration, and delivery. Accreditation is available at three levels:

- LEED Green Associate
- LEED Accredited Professional
- LEED Fellow

GBCI also oversees the development and implementation of a credential maintenance program for LEED Accredited Professionals. Establishing continuing education requirements for LEED Accredited Professionals ensures that the credential continues to distinguish those building professionals who have a thorough understanding of green building principles and practices plus the skills to steward the LEED certification process.

GBCI administers all LEED project certification through third-party certification bodies accredited by the American National Standards Institute (ANSI).

LEED RATING SYSTEMS

The LEED rating systems are tools for encouraging, evaluating, and recognizing green buildings and neighborhoods, with the ultimate goal of market transformation. Comprehensive and flexible, LEED is relevant to buildings in any stage in their life cycles. New construction, the ongoing operations and maintenance of an existing building, and a significant tenant retrofit to a commercial building are all addressed by LEED rating systems. The rating systems and their companion reference guides help teams make the right green building decisions for their projects through an integrated process, ensuring that building systems work together effectively. Updated regularly, the rating systems respond to new technologies and policies and to changes in the built environment through an ongoing, consensus-based refinement process.

The LEED rating systems address the following types and scopes of projects:

- LEED for New Construction and Major Renovation
- LEED for Core & Shell
- LEED for Commercial Interiors
- LEED for Schools
- LEED for Healthcare
- LEED for Retail
- LEED for Existing Buildings: Operations & Maintenance
- LEED for Homes
- LEED for Neighborhood Development

The LEED for New Construction and Major Renovation Rating System, which addresses the full design and construction of most commercial buildings and large (more than four stories) multifamily residential projects, was the first version of LEED to be developed; it has served as the basis for the other rating systems. LEED for Core & Shell is for projects restricted to the design and construction of the core and exterior shell, and LEED for Commercial Interiors addresses only interior design and tenant fit-outs. Each rating system follows a similar structure, with green building strategies divided into the following categories:

- Sustainable Sites
- Water Efficiency
- Energy and Atmosphere
- Materials and Resources
- Indoor Environmental Quality
- Innovation in Design

> A seventh category, Regional Priority, has been developed by USGBC chapters to address regionally important issues, such as water conservation in the Southwest. At the publication of this guide, the details were still being finalized by USGBC.

LEED for Schools, LEED for Healthcare, and LEED for Retail are derivatives of LEED for New Construction and Major Renovation and LEED for Commercial Interiors. These rating systems are customized to the unique nature of each market segment. For example, LEED for Schools provides additional focus on classroom acoustics, master planning, mold prevention, and environmental site assessment. LEED for Retail addresses the types of spaces that retailers need for their distinctive product lines.

LEED for Existing Buildings: Operations & Maintenance focuses on the ongoing operation of existing buildings, rather than on design and construction. This system has the same categories as the above systems but is geared toward the sustainability strategies associated with building operations.

LEED for Homes, for single-family and small multifamily homes, includes two additional categories:

- Location and Linkages
- Awareness and Education

LEED for Neighborhood Development is designed to address the land-use planning of an entire neighborhood, including buildings, infrastructure, street design, and open space. This system, which was developed in partnership with the Congress for New Urbanism and the Natural Resources Defense Council, is organized into entirely different categories:

- Smart Location and Linkage
- Neighborhood Pattern and Design
- Green Infrastructure and Buildings

Prerequisites and Credits

Each category in a LEED rating system consists of prerequisites and credits. Prerequisites are required elements—green building strategies that must be included in any LEED-certified project. Credits are optional elements—strategies that projects can elect to pursue to gain points toward LEED certification. LEED prerequisites and credits work together to provide a common foundation of performance and a flexible set of tools and strategies to accommodate the circumstances of individual projects.

LEED rating systems generally have 100 base points plus 6 Innovation in Design points and 4 Regional Priority points, for a total of 110 points (LEED for Homes is based on a 125-point scale, plus 11 Innovation in Design points). Projects achieve certification if they earn points according to the following levels:

- Certified, 40–49 points
- Silver, 50–59 points
- Gold, 60–79 points
- Platinum, 80+ points

Credit Weightings

Each credit is allocated points based on the relative importance of the building-related impacts that it addresses. The result is a weighted average that combines building impacts and the relative value of the impact categories. Credits that most directly address the most important environmental impacts and human benefits are given the greatest weight; the market implications of point allocation are also considered.

The credit weightings are based on impact categories defined by the U.S. Environmental Protection Agency and on category weights established by the National Institute of Standards and Technology and modified by USGBC. The combination of impact categories and category weights provides a quantitative basis for determining the point value of each credit in the LEED rating systems.

Overall, the credit weights emphasize energy efficiency, renewable energy, reduced transportation demand, and water conservation, based on their direct contribution to reducing high-priority impacts, particularly greenhouse gas emissions.

Figure 2 illustrates the relative importance of impacts based on priorities in the 2009 versions of the LEED rating systems; the height of each bar reflects its relative influence on the distribution of points across the system.

Figure 2. Impact Categories (Source: USGBC LEED 2009 Weightings Workbook)

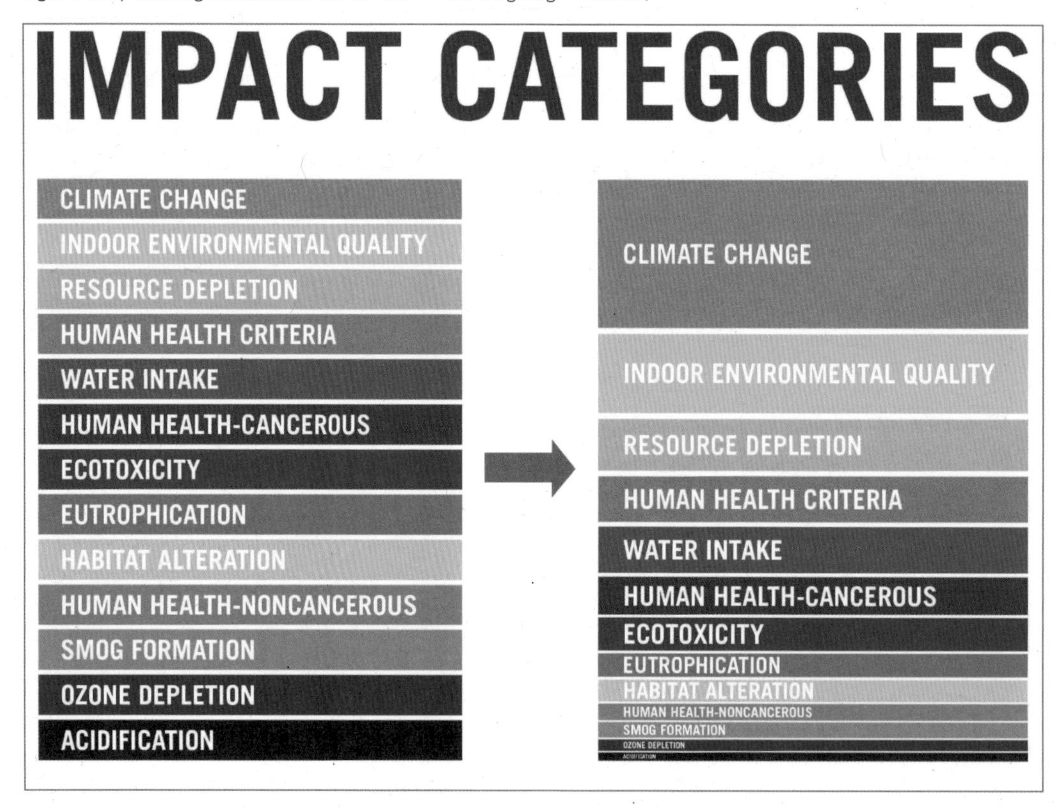

Carbon Overlay

The U.S. Green Building Council is a signatory to the Wingspread Principles on a U.S. Response to Global Warming, a set of propositions signed by individuals and organizations declaring their commitment to addressing the issue of climate change. These principles are based on recognition that global climate change is a critical challenge that requires changes in our economy, policies, and behaviors. The Wingspread Principles call for urgent and effective action to reduce greenhouse gas emissions by 60% to 80% below 1990 levels by midcentury.

LEED-rated buildings typically have lower greenhouse gas emissions than comparable conventionally built structures. However, some green buildings have greater reductions than others, sometimes because of the specific strategies used to achieve LEED certification, and sometimes because of the circumstances of the project, such as its location or source of purchased electricity. Accordingly, USGBC now identifies and prioritizes LEED credits based on their relative value for greenhouse gas emissions reduction. This "carbon overlay" is a quantitative index of the relative importance of individual credits.

The score for each LEED credit is estimated based on the carbon footprint for a typical LEED building. A building's carbon footprint is the total greenhouse gas emissions associated with its construction and operation, which include the following:

- Energy used by building systems;
- Building-related transportation;
- Embodied emissions of water (electricity used to extract, convey, treat, and deliver water);
- Embodied emissions of solid waste (life-cycle emissions associated with solid waste); and
- Embodied emissions of materials (emissions associated with the manufacture and transport of materials).

The carbon footprint for constructing and operating a typical 135,000-square-foot office building is represented in Figure 5, which illustrates the sources of emissions of the annual total of 4,700 metric tons of carbon dioxide equivalent. This distribution can be used to prioritize credits based on their potential to reduce greenhouse gas emissions. The credits addressing the most important emissions sources receive the highest scores in the carbon overlay. The carbon overlay is included in the LEED 2009 workbooks, including LEED for New Construction and Major Renovation, LEED for Operations & Maintenance, and LEED for Neighborhood Development.

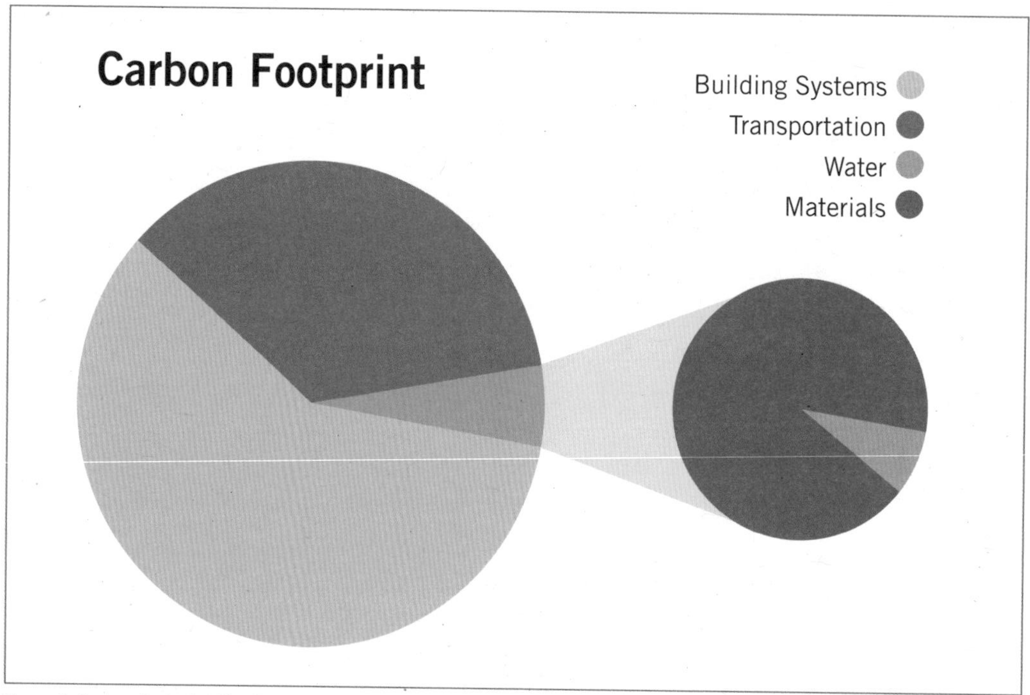

Figure 5. Carbon Footprint Distribution of Typical Office Building (Source: USGBC LEED 2009 Weightings Workbook)

More information about carbon overlays in LEED 2009 is available at http://www.usgbc.org/DisplayPage.aspx?CMSPageID=1849.

THINK ABOUT IT

LEED and greenhouse gas reduction. Many government agencies and organizations have established requirements for LEED certification as a way of meeting their climate change goals. Do green buildings rated with flexible, voluntary standards *always* reduce greenhouse gas emissions? What factors can complicate the relationship between green building and greenhouse gas emissions reduction?

Certification Process

Achieving LEED certification requires satisfying all prerequisites and earning a minimum number of points as described in the applicable rating system. Each LEED rating system corresponds with a LEED reference guide that explains credit criteria, describes the benefits of complying with the credit, and suggests approaches to achieving credit compliance.

The LEED process begins with registration. The project team submits a registration form and a fee to USGBC. Once registered, the team receives information, tools, and communications that will help guide the certification process.

When the team is ready for USGBC to review its application, it submits the appropriate fee, which is based on project square footage, and documentation. Submission of documentation for review can be done in either one or two stages. The team can wait until the building project is complete to submit documentation for all the credits it is pursuing. Or the team can seek review of its design-related prerequisites and credits before completion, and then apply for construction-related credits after the project is finished.

Whether the design and construction credits are submitted together or separately, each credit undergoes one preliminary review. The reviewer may request additional information or clarification. The team then submits final documentation. After completion of the final review, teams may appeal any adverse decisions on individual credits to USGBC for an additional fee.

All projects document credit compliance through LEED-Online, a data collection portal through which the team can upload information about the project. It provides credit templates to be completed and signed by a specified member of the team (architect, engineer, general contractor, landscape architect, owner, etc.). In the near future, LEED-Online will provide dynamic, context-dependent prompts for data collection.

Two LEED rating systems follow slightly different processes, reflecting differences in planning and development.

LEED for Homes involves a multistep review, based on the phases in the design and construction of new homes, with participation by project team members, including a LEED for Homes provider, the homebuilder, a green rater, and a home energy rater. The verification process has five steps:

- **Step 1.** Early planning
- **Step 2.** Design
- **Step 3.** Build
- **Step 4.** Verification and certification
- **Step 5.** Reflection on achievements

LEED for Neighborhood Development follows the typical neighborhood development process—which can take years or even decades—from the earliest steps of project entitlement (acquiring the necessary permits) to the completion of the project. This process is segmented into three stages for review:

- **Stage 1.** Review prior to completion of the entitlement (permitting) process
- **Stage 2.** Certification of an approved development plan
- **Stage 3.** Review of a completed neighborhood development

USGBC provides comprehensive information about the LEED process on its project certification webpage, http://www.usgbc.org/displaypage.aspx?cmspageid=64.

Credit Interpretation

The LEED rating systems are intended to be flexible, voluntary tools to improve the performance of buildings and promote market transformation. Over time, experience with LEED projects has generated findings that document reviewers' responses to questions about credit requirements or their application in specific circumstances. These credit interpretation rulings constitute precedents.

Reviews of thousands of projects have generated a substantial foundation of experience, some of which has been described in case studies. The rulings also indicate how particular credits have been reviewed under different circumstances and whether a team's approach will be acceptable. Project teams must consult rulings and errata that have been posted prior to their registration date and comply with any guidance that applies. Any rulings that are posted following the date of registration may be incorporated if they benefit the team, but reviewers will not hold teams responsible for complying with rulings issued after their registration date.

If a new issue arises, a project team can submit a credit interpretation request. Guidelines for submitting credit interpretation requests are available at http://www.usgbc.org/showfile.aspx?documentid=1510.

SUSTAINABLE SITES

The location of a project is the foundation for the sustainability of individual buildings or an entire neighborhood. The sustainability of a project site has several aspects:

- Transportation;
- Site selection;
- Site design and management; and
- Stormwater management.

These elements encompass the interaction between a project and its local and regional circumstances, as well as the project's impact on ecosystems and water resources. The most sustainable sites are locations that reduce transportation demand, restore degraded or contaminated areas, minimize impacts such as light pollution, and manage stormwater to protect water quality and aquatic ecosystems.

Assessments and Measurements

To evaluate the performance of site-related strategies, the following measures and metrics can be used. Some of these, like community connectivity, are qualitative measures, while others lend themselves to quantitative measurement, such as the solar reflectance rating of a surface or the number of footcandles of lighting.

- **Brownfield.** Previously used or developed land that may be contaminated with hazardous waste or pollution. Once any environmental damage has been remediated, the land can be reused. Redevelopment on brownfields provides an important opportunity to restore degraded urban land while promoting infill and reducing sprawl.
- **Community connectivity.** The amount of connection between a site and the surrounding community, measured by proximity of the site to homes, schools, parks, stores, restaurants, medical facilities, and other services and amenities.
- **Development density.** The total square footage of all buildings within a particular area, measured in square feet per acre or units per acre.
- **Diversity of uses or housing types.** The number of types of spaces or housing types per acre. A neighborhood that includes a diversity of uses—offices, homes, schools, parks, stores—encourages walking, and its residents and visitors are less dependent on personal vehicles. A diversity of housing types allows households of different types, sizes, ages, and incomes to live in the same neighborhood.
- **Floodplain.** Land that is likely to be flooded by a storm of a given size (e.g., a 100-year storm).
- **Floor-area ratio.** The relationship between the total building floor area and the allowable land area the building can cover. In green building, the objective is to build up rather than out because a smaller footprint means less disruption of the existing or created landscape.
- **Footcandle.** A measure of the amount of illumination falling on a surface. A footcandle is equal to one lumen per square foot. Minimizing the number of footcandles of site lighting helps reduce light pollution and protect dark skies and nocturnal animals.
- **Imperviousness.** The resistance of a material to penetration by a liquid. The total imperviousness of a surface, such as paving, is expressed as a percentage of total land area that does not allow moisture penetration. Impervious surfaces prevent rainwater from infiltrating into the ground, thereby increasing runoff, reducing groundwater recharge, and degrading surface water quality.
- **Native and adapted plants.** Native plants occur naturally in a given location and ecosystem. Adapted plants are not native to a location but grow reliably with minimal attention from humans. Using native and adapted plants can reduce the amount of water required for irrigation, as well as the need for pesticides or fertilizers, and may provide benefits for local wildlife.
- **Prime farmland.** Previously undeveloped land with soil suitable for cultivation. Avoiding development on prime farmland helps protect agricultural lands, which are needed for food production.
- **Site disturbance.** The amount of a site that is disturbed by construction activity. On undeveloped sites, limiting the amount and boundary of site disturbance can protect surrounding habitat.
- **Solar reflectance index (SRI).** A measure of how well a material rejects solar heat; the index ranges from 0 (least reflective) to 100 (most reflective). Using "cooler" materials helps prevent the urban heat island effect (the absorption of heat by roofs and pavement and its radiation to the ambient air) and minimizes demand for cooling of nearby buildings.
- **Street grid density.** An indicator of neighborhood density, calculated as the number of centerline miles per square mile. Centerline miles are the length of a road down its center. A

community with high street grid density and narrow, interconnected streets is more likely to be pedestrian friendly than one with a low street grid density and wide streets.

- **Transportation demand management.** The process of reducing peak-period vehicle trips.
- **Vehicle miles traveled (vmt).** A measure of transportation demand that estimates the travel miles associated with a project, most often for single-passenger cars. LEED sometimes uses a complementary metric for alternative-mode miles (e.g., in high-occupancy autos).

THINK ABOUT IT

Green building and transportation. Transportation is a fundamental impact associated with the built environment. What does it mean to have a "green" building in an auto-dependent location? Is consideration of transportation an opportunity or a barrier to projects considering LEED certification?

TRANSPORTATION

According to the U.S. Energy Information Administration, transportation accounted for 32% of total U.S. greenhouse gas emissions in 2007. Buildings generate much of the demand for transportation, and they can be an important part of efforts to reduce the social, economic, and environmental impacts of transportation. Land-use decisions and the design, construction, and operation of buildings can reduce the length and frequency of vehicle trips and encourage shifts to more sustainable modes of transportation.

Considering transportation may be a new issue for many building design professionals. Some owners, architects, engineers, and other professionals have questioned why LEED 2009 increases the emphasis on this issue. Conversely, land-use and transportation planning professionals are often frustrated by claims of "green" buildings in auto-dependent locations.

LEED recognizes that creating a building or neighborhood can create new demand for transportation; however, projects also have opportunities to reduce transportation impacts by using a wide variety of practical strategies, such as providing alternative modes of transportation, encouraging walking and bicycling, providing fueling facilities for alternative-fuel vehicles, and reducing the number and length of automobile trips. Taken together, these strategies can significantly reduce the impacts of building-associated transportation.

The drivers of transportation impacts include location, vehicle technology, fuel, and human behavior. Location determines the number and frequency of trips. Vehicle technology determines the quantity and types of energy and support systems needed to convey people and goods to and from the site. Fuel determines the environmental impact of vehicle operation. Human behavior ultimately combines all of these elements in daily mobility choices. Green building's emphasis on integrative approaches calls for the coordinated, synergistic consideration for each of these elements.

In practice, green building often assesses the elements of transportation through proxy measures and metrics. For example, density stands in for many elements of land-use design. Project sites in urban areas are likely to have the density required for the sustainable operation of mass transportation—systems that are less energy intensive than single-passenger vehicles. By building in a relatively high density area or on an infill site already served by mass transit, the project can reduce the vehicle miles traveled by its occupants and visitors and more easily integrate into existing transportation networks.

> Sites without access to public transportation start at a disadvantage and may require additional attention to transportation impacts, particularly local land-use design and alternative fuels. It is still possible for such a project to substantially reduce its transportation impacts by focusing on local connectivity and the energy efficiency of the vehicles used to serve its needs. For example, an office complex without transit access might provide incentives for carpooling, incorporate diverse land uses that allow workers to walk to basic services, or facilitate the use of alternative-fuel vehicles like plug-in hybrids.

Consideration for transportation provides many opportunities for integrative planning, such as specifications for parking. Typically, parking is sized for annual extreme events, like shopping on the day after Thanksgiving; during the other 364 days of the year, parking capacity is unused, and unnecessary expanses of asphalt or concrete have environmental impacts, causing urban heat islands and stormwater runoff. A project team can reduce the number of parking spaces provided for single-passenger vehicles, thereby discouraging vehicle use, reducing environmental impacts, and lowering the cost of construction. Project teams can go further and designate preferred parking spaces for alternative-fuel vehicles. Incentives for low-impact behavior may become more appealing as technologies like plug-in hybrids become more common.

Promoting alternative transportation as a convenient and viable option through site selection, design, and incentives benefits both the building occupants and the developer. Recognizing the importance of alternative transportation in reducing negative environmental impacts, the LEED rating systems include multiple credits that give project teams flexibility when considering site-specific needs and opportunities.

Strategies to address transportation include the following:

- **Locate near mass transit.** Select a project site in an area served by an existing transportation network.
- **Limit parking.** The lack of parking spaces on the project site will spark interest in alternative transportation options.
- **Encourage carpooling.** Designate preferred spaces for carpool vehicles in the parking area.
- **Promote alternative-fuel vehicles.** Provide a convenient refueling station on the site.
- **Offer incentives.** Develop an alternative commuting incentive program for building occupants.
- **Support alternative transportation.** Promote alternatives to single-occupancy car commuting at the building and/or city level.

Primary Resources: Transportation, Energy, and Greenhouse Gas Emissions

Greenhouse gas emissions from transportation are the result of three fundamental factors: vehicle technology, transportation fuels, and land use.

Although efforts are underway to improve vehicle fuel efficiency and reduce the carbon intensity of motor fuels, recent research suggests that these efforts may be insufficient to meet greenhouse gas reduction goals without significant changes in land use. Land use is what ultimately drives growth in transportation demand, and urban sprawl is increasing transportation demand faster than vehicles and fuels can improve. The result may be a net increase in greenhouse gas emissions despite substantial investments in technology and alternative energy. Green building professionals can help prevent this outcome by helping reduce transportation demand and slow or reverse the long-term growth in vehicle miles traveled.

- Commuting guide for employers, www.self-propelled-city.com.
- *Growing Cooler: The Evidence on Urban Development and Climate Change,* by Reid Ewing, Keith Bartholomew, Steve Winkelman, Jerry Walters, and Don Chen (Urban Land Institute, 2008)
- Smart commuting, www.smartcomute.org.

THINK ABOUT IT

Electric cars and net-zero buildings. Buildings create the demand for transportation. In the future, they may also supply the energy to fuel our transportation system. What are the implications of the growing convergence between vehicles and buildings? How will electrification of vehicles transform transportation *and* buildings? How might it alter energy efficiency or onsite renewable energy goals for buildings?

SITE SELECTION

The selection of a project site can provide opportunities to protect habitat and restore degraded areas. Development or redevelopment on former industrial properties (so-called brownfields) may require the cleanup of contaminated soil or groundwater. Brownfield redevelopment can be regenerative: it improves the quality of the environment. This strategy also reduces pressure for the development of greenfield (undeveloped) sites, which in turn reduces fragmentation of natural habitats. Some projects take the extra step of explicitly protecting additional habitat outside the project boundaries as part of the development process.

Strategies to address site selection include the following:

- **Increase density.** Create a smaller footprint and maximize the floor-area ratio or square footage per acre.
- **Choose redevelopment.** Build on a previously developed or brownfield site.
- **Protect habitat.** Give preference to locations that do not include sensitive site elements and land types.

LEED in Practice

Smart locations and LEED for Neighborhood Development

LEED for Neighborhood Development encourages development within and near existing communities or public transportation infrastructure. The goal is to reduce vehicle trips and miles traveled and support walking as a transportation choice. This promotes public health and a vibrant community life.

One measure of "smart location" is access to transit service. LEED recognizes projects that locate at least 50% of dwelling unit entrances within a 1/4 -mile walk of bus or streetcar stops or a 1/2 -mile walk from bus rapid transit, light or heavy passenger rail stations, ferry terminals, or tram terminals.

The variation in distances reflects repeated observations that residents are willing to walk farther to reach certain types of transit.

For more information, see the LEED for Neighborhood Development Rating System, Smart Location and Linkage, Prerequisite 1, Smart Location.

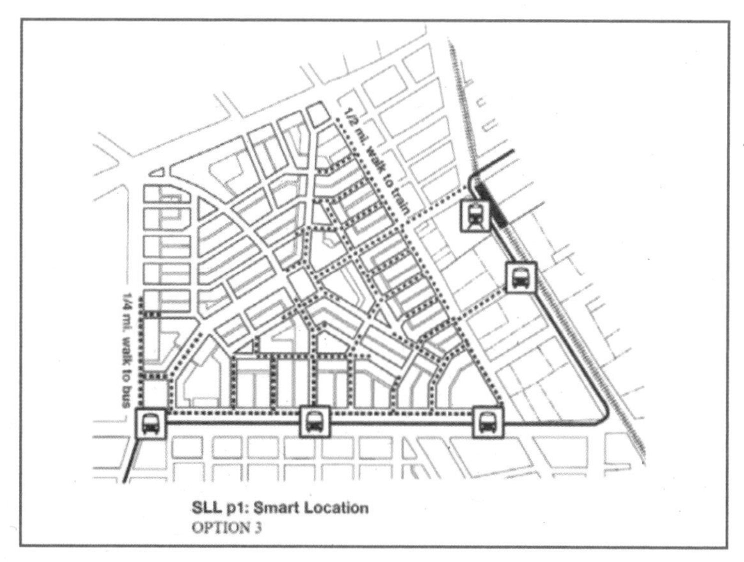

Figure 6. Measuring Walking Distance to Public Transportation (Source: USGBC LEED for Neighborhood Development)
A distance of one-half mile or less is one measure of a "smart" location.

Primary Resources: Brownfields

EPA defines brownfields as "real property, the expansion, redevelopment, or reuse of which may be complicated by the presence or potential presence of a hazardous substance, pollutant, or contaminant." If found to be contaminated but then remediated, the land can be reused. Cleaning up and reinvesting in these properties takes development pressure off undeveloped land, and it both improves and protects the environment.

Brownfields provide exceptional opportunities for green building projects to go beyond just reducing their impacts on the environment. Restoration of brownfields can also be regenerative and actually improve social, economic, and environmental conditions. Encouraging regenerative projects is a long-term goal of USGBC. EPA worked with USGBC to help recognize and reward projects that choose brownfields with points in the LEED rating systems.

EPA offers a variety of resources for brownfield redevelopment:

- Brownfields and land revitalization grants and funding, http://www.epa.gov/swerosps/bf/pilot.htm.
- Tools and technical information related to brownfield cleanup, http://www.epa.gov/swerosps/bf/toolsandtech.htm.
- Interactive maps of brownfield cleanup sites across the United States, http://iaspub.epa.gov/Clea nups/.

THINK ABOUT IT

Regenerative design. Buildings have traditionally been seen as having adverse impacts on the environment. In fact, the whole concept of environmental impact assessment often presumes that development has a net negative impact. What are the implications of regenerative planning and design for environmental policy in the United States?

SITE DESIGN AND MANAGEMENT

Sustainable landscapes reduce environmental impacts, minimize maintenance costs, and contribute to the restoration and regeneration of an area. Projects often achieve these goals by incorporating native and adapted plants, using water-efficient irrigation systems, minimizing impervious area, and improving outdoor lighting design. Certain plants can enhance soil nutrients and deter pests. Plants can also be selected to minimize evapotranspiration and create wildlife habitat for pest predators. Landscape design can thereby stabilize the soil and reduce or eliminate the need for irrigation, pesticides, and fertilizers.

Strategically locating functional and/or decorative hardscape on a project site may reduce the amount of impervious area and site lighting required to provide adequate illumination while preserving the integrity of the night sky. The choice of roofing and paving materials can accomplish multiple purposes. For example, during the day the use of reflective materials (those with high SRI values) contributes to reducing heat gain and peak air temperatures. This increases comfort and reduces demand for air-conditioning. In the evening, reflective materials help distribute light across the site, reducing the number of fixtures needed to safely illuminate the area and saving energy.

Strategies for developing a sustainable site design include the following:

- **Build small.** Minimize the building footprint and maximize open space.
- **Minimize hardscape.** Design driveways and paths intelligently, or substitute permeable surfaces for traditional paving.
- **Minimize water usage.** Install water-efficient irrigation systems that use nonpotable water and evapotranspiration controllers, or design a landscape that needs no irrigation.
- **Use reflective materials.** Specify exterior surfaces with high SRI values to enhance illumination levels and reduce heat island impacts.
- **Develop a sustainable management plan.** The plan should address the application of chemicals and the cleaning of hardscape and building exterior, and it should include an integrated pest management program.

STORMWATER MANAGEMENT

Precipitation is part of the natural hydrologic cycle, but uncontrolled stormwater is a major problem.

Conventional new development often increases the expanse of impervious surfaces and creates new sources of pollution, like fertilized landscape plantings. Impervious materials prevent the percolation and infiltration of stormwater runoff, which then rushes off the site, causing soil erosion and sedimentation in local waterways. This runoff can also carry harmful chemicals into the water system, deteriorating surface water quality and harming aquatic life and recreation opportunities in receiving waters.

> LEED recognizes and encourages planning, design, and operational practices that control stormwater and protect the quality of surface and ground water. This begins with land-use plans that limit the extent of impervious surface area, often through local increases in density and the protection of natural habitat and ecosystems. It continues with the use of structural and site design features that slow and retain water onsite, providing more time for natural infiltration and contributing to more natural hydrologic conditions.

Stormwater management can also include the collection and reuse of this water for nonpotable uses, such as landscape irrigation, toilet and urinal flushing, and custodial uses. This helps reduce stormwater runoff while also avoiding the unnecessary consumption of expensive and energy-intensive potable water.

Many water resource issues involve local rules and regional environmental conditions. For example, in the eastern United States, onsite water collection is often encouraged as part of efforts to slow stormwater runoff and reduce nonpoint source pollution. Conversely, in some western states, long-standing water laws prohibit onsite water collection because the water is obligated to downstream users.

Strategies for controlling and reducing stormwater runoff include the following:

- **Minimize impervious areas.** Increase the area of permeable surfaces, such as vegetated roofs, porous pavement, and grid pavers.
- **Control stormwater.** Direct runoff into dry ponds, rain gardens, bioswales, and similar landscaping features designed to hold water and slow the rate of runoff.
- **Harvest rainwater.** In many jurisdictions, the water collected can be used in building systems, such as toilets or irrigation.

Primary Resources: Low-Impact Development

A hard rain cleans the streets—and that's the problem. Precipitation falling on hard surfaces does not infiltrate and recharge groundwater. Rather, it moves quickly, entraining contaminants and conveying them into rivers and streams. EPA calls this nonpoint source pollution, and it is one of the biggest threats to surface water quality and aquatic ecosystems.

Low-impact development (LID) comprises a set of strategies that address how water enters a site, is stored, and ultimately leaves the site. LID minimizes impervious surfaces, protects soils, enhances native vegetation, and manages stormwater at its source.

There are many types of LID programs, but they typically focus on a core set of strategies. For example, the Department of Environmental Resources in Prince George's County, Maryland, uses a design approach that integrates five components: site planning, hydrologic analysis, integrated management practices, erosion and sediment control, and public outreach. This integrated design approach protects surface water by managing stormwater onsite and creating buffers between development and water resources.

- *Low-Impact Development Design Strategies: An Integrated Design Approach* (U.S. EPA, 1999), http://www.epa.gov/owow/nps/lid/lidnatl.pdf.

Some of the design elements identified in LID strategies must be coordinated and balanced with other elements of neighborhood or community design. For example, LEED for Neighborhood Development encourages street grids to promote walkability and reduce auto dependence. However, a conventional street grid may increase total impervious surface area relative to potential alternative designs. LEED for Neighborhood Development encourages projects to balance small-scale stormwater management features with the regional benefits of compact development patterns. Creating compact, high-density development patterns is one strategy to prevent sprawl, which spreads impervious surfaces across larger areas: impermeability may increase within high-density centers but is minimized across entire watersheds.

Green building professionals must understand the trade-offs of stormwater management, recognize the full range of available strategies, and apply the combination of approaches that best achieve the intent of protecting water quality and aquatic ecosystems for any specific project.

Stormwater Management

- LEED for Neighborhood Development, http://www.usgbc.org/DisplayPage.aspx?CMSPageID=148.
- Low-impact development (LID) (U.S. EPA), http://www.epa.gov/nps/lid/.
- Stormwater strategies (Natural Resources Defense Council, 1999), http://www.nrdc.org/water/pollution/storm/stoinx.asp.
- Urban Stormwater Management in the United States (National Research Council, 2008), http://www.nap.edu/catalog.php?record_id=12465.

Heat Island Effect

- Alternative paving materials, www.cleanaircounts.org/Resources%20Package/A%20Book/Paving/other%20pavings/coolpave.htm.
- Cool Colors Project (Lawrence Berkeley National Laboratory), www.coolcolors.lbl.gov/.
- Heat island effect (U.S. EPA), www.epa.gov/heatisland.

WATER EFFICIENCY

Americans' use of the limited public water supply continues to increase as development expands. Municipally provided potable water is delivered to users for domestic, commercial, industrial, and other purposes and is the primary source of water for most buildings, but high demand is straining limited supplies. The resulting wastewater then overwhelms treatment facilities, and the untreated overflow can contaminate rivers, lakes, and sources of potable water with bacteria, nitrogen, toxic metals, and other contaminants. Additional municipal supply and treatment facilities must then be built, at public cost.

LEED encourages and recognizes efficiency measures that significantly reduce the amount of potable water used by buildings while still meeting the needs of the systems and the occupants. These measures involve all the water usage associated with buildings:

- Indoor water for restrooms;
- Outdoor water for landscaping; and
- Process water for industrial purposes and building systems.

Efficiency strategies, combined with monitoring that tracks water consumption and identifies problems, can dramatically improve water conservation compared with comparable conventional buildings. Many LEED-rated buildings reduce potable water use by more than 50%, with direct benefits for the bottom line and the environment.

Assessments and Measurements

- **Design versus Baseline.** The amount of water the design case conserves versus the baseline case. All LEED Water Efficiency credits use a baseline case against which the facility's design case is compared. The baseline case represents the Energy Policy Act of 1992 (EPAct 1992) flow and flush rates.
- **Gallons per flush (gpf).** The amount of water consumed by flush fixtures (water closets, or toilets, and urinals). The baseline flush rate for water closets is 1.6 gpf, and for urinals, 1.0 gpf (EPAct 1992).
- **Gallons per minute (gpm).** The amount of water consumed by flow fixtures (lavatory faucets, showerheads, aerators, sprinkler heads).
- **Irrigation efficiency.** The percentage of water delivered by irrigation equipment that is actually used for irrigation and does not evaporate, blow away, or fall on hardscape. For example, overhead spray sprinklers have lower irrigation efficiencies (65%) than drip systems (90%).

INDOOR WATER

Indoor water use refers to the water that occupied buildings typically need to operate on a day-to-day basis—water for water closets, urinals, lavatories, showers, and kitchen or break-room sinks. Indoor water use reduction can be achieved by installing water-efficient fixtures, using nonpotable water for flush functions, and installing submeters to track and log water use trends.

> Low-flow fixtures use less water than specified in the EPAct 1992 requirements. Low-flow models are now available for all indoor plumbing fixtures. Projects can further reduce their potable water consumption by designing and installing plumbing systems that can use captured rainwater or graywater in flush fixtures.

Submetering gives commercial building projects a way to monitor water use, track fixture performance, and identify problems. With submeters, teams can better understand how much water is being used for plumbing fixtures, as well as be alerted to any leaks or other problems that waste water.

Strategies for reducing indoor water use:

- **Install efficient plumbing fixtures.** Replace water-intensive fixtures with new low-flow fixtures. If porcelain replacement proves cost-prohibitive, install new flush valves or flow restrictors (for example, aerators) to achieve water savings.
- **Use nonpotable water.** Strive to use the right water for the right purpose, including captured rainwater, graywater, or municipal reclaimed water for flush fixtures.
- **Install submeters.** Meter indoor water systems and monitor the data to track consumption trends and pinpoint leaks.

Primary Resources: Water Usage in Buildings

The U.S. Geological Survey estimates that the United States uses 400 billion gallons of water per day. The operation of buildings, including landscaping, accounts for approximately 47 billion gallons per day—12% of total water use.

The value of any particular measure for overall water conservation efforts depends on the distribution of end uses—the points of consumption—in a given building. For example, office buildings typically lack extensive laundry and kitchen facilities, and water is used for HVAC systems, restrooms, and landscaping. In contrast, kitchen sinks and dishwashers dominate the end use for restaurants. A water end-use profile can help project teams identify the largest users of water and evaluate the cost-effectiveness of specific conservation strategies, whether it's low-flow fixtures, irrigation technology, or efficient cooling tower systems.

- "Water: Doing More With Less," (*Environmental Building News,* 2008), http://www.buildinggreen.com/auth/article.cfm/ID/3829/.
- *Residential End Uses of Water* (American Water Works Association Research Foundation, 1999), http://www.aquacraft.com/Publications/resident.htm.

THINK ABOUT IT

Waterless urinals. Non-water-using urinals are the ultimate low-flow fixtures. What might be some reasons they are not specified for every new commercial building project?

OUTDOOR WATER

Landscape irrigation is a significant component of many commercial buildings' water use and thus an opportunity to conserve water. A reduction in irrigation water use can be achieved by specifying water-wise landscaping and water-efficient irrigation technology, using nonpotable water for irrigation, and installing submeters to track and log irrigation trends.

Project teams should incorporate native and adapted species in the landscape design, because these plants tend to thrive without irrigation, pesticides, or fertilizer. Drought-tolerant and xeriscape plantings are also preferable because of their extremely low water needs.

High-performance irrigation systems include efficient water supply and control technology, such as drip and bubbler distribution systems and weather-based irrigation controllers, which respond to weather conditions. Potable water use for irrigation can be further reduced by using nonpotable water—harvested rainwater, graywater, or municipal reclaimed water.

Submetering is a way to determine how much water is being used for irrigation purposes. Metering irrigation water can even provide an immediate economic benefit because facilities can receive credit from the utility company for sewer charges, given that the water is not entering the sewer system.

Strategies for reducing outdoor water use:

- **Choose locally adapted plants.** Landscape with native and adapted plants that require less water.
- **Use xeriscaping.** Especially in arid regions, employ xeriscape principles when designing the site landscape.
- **Select efficient irrigation technologies.** Drip and bubbler systems and weather-based controllers can save water.
- **Use nonpotable water.** Match irrigation with the right water, including captured rainwater, graywater, or municipal reclaimed water.
- **Install submeters.** Meter the irrigation system to track consumption and identify leaks.

THINK ABOUT IT

Green lawns and green buildings. Many commercial building landscapes include some turf, yet most of these spaces are not intended for picnics or play. Since turf tends to be water intensive, why is it the go-to choice for landscapes? Why has it become the "baseline" plant material? Why does it cover so many median strips? Why should it not?

PROCESS WATER

Process water is used for industrial processes and building systems, such as cooling towers, boilers, and chillers. These systems provide heat, cool air and water for building operations. Process water also includes the water used for certain business operations (such as washing machines and dishwashers).

Commercial building projects can reduce process water use by selecting efficient cooling towers, chillers, boilers, and other equipment, and by integrating harvested rainwater and nonpotable water to work in conjunction with the specified equipment.

Since process water volumes can be significant, understanding how that water is being used is important. Teams can install submeters on each of the major water-using systems to find out where the water is going and where they should focus their conservation efforts. Metering cooling tower makeup water (water lost to evaporation during cooling tower operation) is particularly important because facilities may be able to receive credit from the utility company for sewer charges, since the water is not entering the sewer system.

Strategies for reducing process water use:

- **Use nonpotable water.** Use the right water for the right purpose. Investigate opportunities to use captured rainwater, graywater, or municipally reclaimed water in building processes and systems, such as cooling towers.
- **Install submeters.** Meter the process water systems and use the data to track consumption and identify leaks.

Primary Resources

- "A 'Green Option' for Cooling Tower Biological Control" *Process Cooling,* (November 2007), www.process-cooling.com/articles/Feature_Article/BNP_GUID_9-5-2006_A_10000000000000214768.
- www.plantnative.org.
- "Water Conservation Guidelines for Cooling Towers" (Sydney Water Board, Australia, no date), www.sydneywater.com.au/Publications/FactSheets/SavingsWaterBestPracticeGuidelinesCoolingTowers.pdf.
- *Water Efficiency, The Journal for Water Conservation Professionals*, http://www.waterefficiency.net/index.aspx.
- "Water Efficiency: The Next Generation," by Scott Chaplin (Rocky Mountain Institute, 1998), http://www.rmi.org/images/PDFs/Water/W98-07_WatEffNxtGen.pdf.
- "Water-Efficient Gardening and Landscaping," by Denny Schrock (University of Missouri Extension, no date), http://muextension.missouri.edu/xplor/agguides/hort/g06912.htm.
- Water Measurement Manual (U.S. Bureau of Reclamation, no date), www.usbr.gov/pmts/hydraulics_lab/pubs/wmm/.
- WaterSense Program (U.S. EPA), www.epa.gov/watersense.

ENERGY AND ATMOSPHERE

Energy has emerged as a critical economic issue and top priority for policymakers. Unsustainable patterns of energy supply and demand have serious implications and long-term impacts on everything from household budgets to international relations. Buildings are on the front line of this issue, and the integrated design of buildings, neighborhoods, and entire communities can dramatically boost energy efficiency and benefit from cleaner, renewable energy supplies. Studies have repeatedly shown that well-designed buildings and land use offer some of the most cost-effective opportunities to save money while reducing greenhouse gas emissions.

Efforts to address energy through green building focus on four interconnected elements:

- Energy demand;
- Energy efficiency;
- Renewable energy; and
- Ongoing energy performance.

Integrative design processes can bring these elements together to identify synergistic strategies. The analysis of whole-building life-cycle costs is central to green building practice because it provides a framework for understanding trade-offs between the first costs and the long-term operating costs of HVAC and other energy-using systems. LEED encourages project teams to use simulation models to quantitatively analyze the trade-offs and identify cost-effective energy-saving strategies. This saves money over the life of the building, saves energy, and reduces greenhouse gas emissions and other environmental impacts.

Assessments and Measurements

- **Energy or greenhouse gas emissions per capita.** A community's total greenhouse gas emissions divided by the total number of residents.
- **Energy use intensity.** Energy consumption divided by the number of square feet in a building, often expressed as British thermal units (Btus) per square foot or as kilowatt-hours of electricity per square foot per year (kWh/sf/yr).
- **Lighting power density.** The installed lighting power per unit area.
- **Measures of energy use.** Typical primary measures of energy consumption associated with buildings include kilowatt-hours of electricity, therms of natural gas, and gallons of liquid fuel.
- **Performance relative to benchmark.** A comparison of a building system's performance with a standard, such as ENERGY STAR Portfolio Manager.
- **Performance relative to code.** A comparison of a building system's performance with a baseline that is equivalent to minimal compliance with an applicable energy code, such as ASHRAE Standard 90 or California's Title 24.

ENERGY DEMAND

Saving energy begins with reducing energy demand. Green buildings and neighborhoods can reduce demand for energy by capturing natural, incidental energy, such as sunlight, wind, and geothermal potential, and by using integrated design processes to reduce loads. Examples include the following:

- Roads, infrastructure, and parcels can be configured so that buildings minimize solar gain in summer and maximize it in winter.
- Adjacent buildings can be designed to shade and insulate each other.
- Building designs can incorporate passive strategies, such as mass and daylight, to reduce the demand for artificial lighting, heating, and cooling.
- Project teams can incorporate technologies and processes that encourage occupants to understand and reduce their individual and aggregate energy demand.

Taken together, demand reduction strategies provide the foundation for energy efficiency and the effective use of renewable energy.

Strategies for reducing energy demand include the following:

- **Establish design and energy goals.** Set targets and establish performance indicators at the outset of a project and periodically verify their achievement.
- **Size the building appropriately.** A facility that is larger than necessary to serve its function creates costly and unproductive energy demand.
- **Use free energy.** Orient the facility to take advantage of natural ventilation, solar energy, and daylighting.
- **Insulate.** Design the building envelope to insulate efficiently against heating and cooling losses.
- **Monitor consumption.** Use energy monitoring and feedback systems to encourage occupants to reduce energy demand.

LEED in Practice

Reducing Demand by Reducing Building Size

Energy demand typically increases directly with building size: The more square feet in a building, the more energy it consumes. Although this is not always true, the relationship between square footage and consumption is very strong.

The LEED for Homes Rating System includes an adjustment to compensate for the effect of square footage on resource consumption by adjusting the point thresholds for the Certified, Silver, Gold, and Platinum ratings based on home size (Figure 7). The adjustment applies to all LEED for Homes credits, not just to strategies related to Energy and Atmosphere.

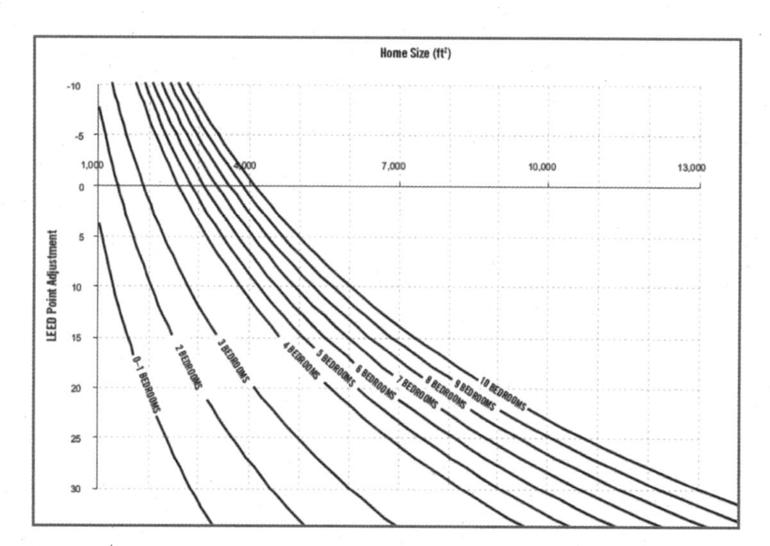

Figure 7. Home Size Adjustment Chart for LEED for Homes

The adjustment explicitly accounts for the material and energy impacts of home construction and operation: Depending on the design, location, and occupants of the home, a 100% increase in home size yields an increase in annual energy use of 15% to 50% and an increase in materials usage of 40% to 90%. LEED for Homes is currently the only LEED rating system with this type of adjustment.

ENERGY EFFICIENCY

Efforts to reduce energy demand provide the foundation for efforts to use energy efficiently. This means getting the most productive work from a unit of energy—often described as a measure of energy intensity. Common metrics for buildings and neighborhoods include energy use per square foot and use per capita.

Buildings need to provide efficient space conditioning, water heating, lighting, refrigeration, conveyance (elevators and escalators), and safety (see the energy end-use profile developed by the EPA for a typical office building, represented in Figure 8). Green building emphasizes an integrated approach to addressing these issues through whole-building design.

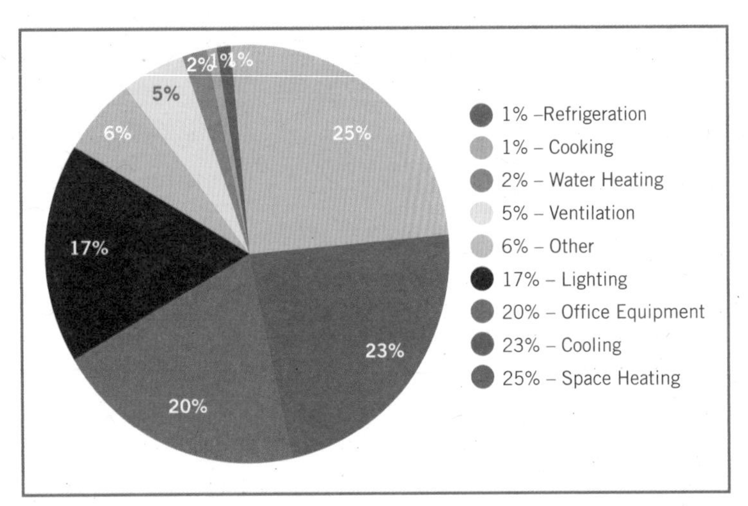

Figure 8. Energy End Uses in Typical Office Building (Source: Data from U.S. EPA Green Building Working Group)

For example, green building project teams can identify opportunities to improve building envelopes (windows, walls, and roof) in ways that enable them to reduce or even eliminate HVAC systems. This kind of integrated design can reduce both initial capital costs and long-term operating costs.

Strategies for achieving energy efficiency include the following:

- **Identify passive design opportunities.** Use the natural resources of sun and wind to heat, cool, and illuminate a building without additional energy. Proper building orientation, selection of materials, and location of windows can allow a building to be warm in the winter, stay cool in the summer, and capture daylight.
- **Address the envelope.** Use the regionally appropriate amount of insulation in the walls and roof and install high-performance glazing to minimize unwanted heat gain or loss. Make sure that the building is properly weatherized.
- **Install high-performance mechanical systems.** Apply life-cycle analysis to the trade-offs between capital and operating costs, and evaluate investments in energy efficiency technologies accordingly.
- **Specify high-efficiency appliances.** Computers, monitors, printers, and microwave ovens that meet or exceed ENERGY STAR requirements will reduce plug load demands (that is, electrical loads associated with plug-in appliances).
- **Use high-efficiency infrastructure.** Efficient street lighting and LED-based traffic signals will reduce energy demands from neighborhood infrastructure.
- **Capture efficiencies of scale.** Design district heating and cooling systems, in which multiple buildings are part of a single loop.

- **Use thermal energy storage.** Generating ice at night, to be used for cooling during the day, takes advantage of off-peak energy, which is cheaper and often cleaner because some utility companies run their older, dirtier generators only to meet peak demand.
- **Use energy simulation.** Computer modeling can identify and prioritize energy efficiency opportunities.
- **Monitor and verify performance.** Ensure that the building systems are functioning as designed and in support of the owner's project requirements through control systems, a building automation system, and commissioning and retrocommissioning.

LEED in Practice

LEED for New Construction and Major Renovation requires new buildings to exceed baseline energy performance standards. One option for complying with LEED requirements involves conducting a whole-building energy simulation, in which the building is represented in a computer program and compared with a baseline building that complies with Appendix G of ASHRAE Standard 90.1.

When running an energy simulation model, project teams distinguish between regulated and process energy.

> Regulated energy powers lighting (interior, parking garage, surface parking, façades, building grounds), HVAC (space heating, cooling, fans, pumps, toilet exhaust, parking garage ventilation), and service water heating (domestic or space heating). This energy is subject to LEED's minimum performance requirements.

Process energy runs office equipment, computers, elevators and escalators, kitchen cooking and refrigeration units, laundry washers and dryers, lighting that is exempt from the lighting power allowance (for example, lighting integral to medical equipment), and miscellaneous items (such as, waterfall pumps). Process energy is not subject to the LEED minimum performance requirements.

For more information, see LEED for New Construction and Major Renovation, Energy and Atmosphere Credit 1, Optimize Energy Performance.

Primary Resources: Energy Performance of LEED Buildings

On average, green buildings provide superior energy efficiency, thereby reducing a wide range of environmental impacts, saving operating costs, and contributing to greenhouse gas emissions reduction goals. Green buildings have also provided new information on the real-world performance of buildings—information that clearly demonstrates the importance of building commissioning and monitoring.

The New Buildings Institute investigated 121 commercial office buildings certified in the United States under LEED for New Construction and Major Renovation and found that they used 24% less energy than the national average. Almost half of the buildings achieved an ENERGY STAR Portfolio Manager score of 75 or above, with an overall average score of 68 (a score of 50 represents average building performance). However, the study also collected data suggesting that a significant percentage of buildings underperformed their benchmarks.

This last finding reinforces the need to commission systems and monitor performance over time so that green buildings can achieve their full potential.

- "Assessing Green Building Performance: A Post Occupancy Evaluation of 12 GSA Buildings" (U.S. General Services Administration, 2008), http://www.gsa.gov/Portal/gsa/ep/contentView.do?contentType=GSA_BASIC&contentId=25545&noc=T.
- "The Energy Challenge: A New Agenda for Corporate Real Estate" (Rocky Mountain Institute and CoreNet Global, 2007), http://www.usgbccolorado.com/news-events/documents/Energy-Challenge.pdf.
- "Energy Performance of LEED for New Construction Buildings," by Cathy Turner and Mark Frankel (New Buildings Institute, 2008), http://www.newbuildings.org/downloads/Energy_Performance_of_LEED-NC_Buildings-Final_3-4-08b.pdf.
- "Lessons Learned from Case Studies of Six High-Performance Buildings," by P. Torcellini et al. (National Renewable Energy Laboratory, 2006), http://www.nrel.gov/docs/fy06osti/37542.pdf.

Refrigerants

Refrigerants, which cost-effectively transfer thermal energy in air-conditioning and refrigeration systems, have remarkable functional properties. They also have damaging side effects on the environment. The choice of refrigerants for building systems poses trade-offs between performance, depletion of stratospheric ozone, and contributions to global warming.

The Montreal Protocol bans the production of chlorofluorocarbon (CFC) refrigerants and phases out hydrochlorofluorocarbon (HCFC) refrigerants to conserve stratospheric ozone—a gas that protects human health and the environment by absorbing harmful UV radiation. Although substitutes possess dramatically lower ozone-depleting power (that is, the degree to which a chemical over its lifetime destroys stratospheric ozone over its lifetime in the atmosphere), they are often potent greenhouse gases. Additionally, replacement refrigerants are somewhat less efficient as working fluids, making cooling systems use more energy per unit of cooling output.

To achieve LEED certification, new buildings may not use CFC-based refrigerants, and existing buildings must complete a total CFC phase-out prior to project completion. LEED awards points for projects that entirely avoid the use of refrigerants or select refrigerants that balance concerns about ozone depletion and global warming. LEED recognizes that there are no perfect refrigerants but it is possible to carefully consider performance characteristics and overall environmental impacts and select a refrigerant with an acceptable trade-off.

- "The Treatment by LEED of the Environmental Impact of HVAC Refrigerants" (USGBC Technical and Scientific Advisory Committee, 2004), http://www.usgbc.org/Docs/LEED_tsac/TSAC_Refrig_Report_Final-Approved.pdf.

RENEWABLE ENERGY

Reduced demand and increased efficiency often make it cost-effective to meet most or all of a building's energy needs from renewable sources. Renewable energy is typically understood to include solar, wind, wave, biomass, and geothermal power, plus certain forms of hydropower. Use of these energy sources avoids the myriad environmental impacts associated with the production and consumption of traditional fuels, such as coal, nuclear power, oil, and natural gas.

LEED distinguishes between onsite renewable energy production and the purchase of offsite green power. Onsite energy production typically involves a system that generates clean electricity, such as solar photovoltaic panels that convert light energy into electricity. Offsite renewable energy is purchased from a utility or a provider of renewable energy certificates (RECs). Sometimes projects can enter into agreements that provide for specific energy sources, such as wind or biomass, from a particular generation facility. A project usually pays a premium for green power.

Strategies for meeting energy demand with renewable energy include the following:

- **Generate onsite renewable energy.** Install photovoltaic cells, solar hot-water heaters, or building-mounted wind turbines.
- **Purchase offsite renewable energy.** Buy green power or renewable energy certificates to reduce the impact of purchased electricity and promote renewable energy generation.

ONGOING ENERGY PERFORMANCE

Attention to energy use doesn't end with the design and construction of an energy-efficient building or neighborhood. It is critical to ensure that a project functions as designed and that it sustains and improves this performance over time. LEED recognizes and encourages operational energy performance through its requirements for building commissioning and credits for monitoring and verification.

Analogous to the commissioning of a new ship, building commissioning ensures that a new building functions as designed. This detailed process begins early in the design phase, with the specification of requirements. Consideration for these requirements is carried through the entire building design and construction process, and the requirements are used as the basis for evaluating performance. Continual commissioning, an ongoing part of building operations, ensures that a building always meets its fundamental operational requirements. Retrocommissioning is the same process applied to existing buildings; it is intended to return the building to its original operational goals—and sometimes exceed them.

Monitoring and verification provide the basis for tracking energy performance with the goal of identifying and resolving any problems that may arise over time. Monitoring often involves comparing building performance measurements with predictions from a calibrated energy simulation or industry benchmarking tool. The EPA's ENERGY STAR Portfolio Manager is one of the most widely used benchmarking systems. Portfolio Manager users enter data on electricity and natural gas consumption, along with other supporting information, into a Web-based tool. The system then evaluates the performance of the building against that of others with similar characteristics. This is an exceptionally useful, free tool for gauging the relative performance of buildings.

Strategies for maintaining energy efficiency include the following:

- **Adhere to owner's project requirements.** Prepare detailed owner's project requirements at the beginning of the design process and conduct commissioning throughout the life cycle of the project to ensure that the building functions as designed.
- **Provide staff training.** Knowledge and training empower facility managers to improve the performance of buildings over time.
- **Conduct preventive maintenance.** Develop a robust preventive maintenance program to keep the building in optimal condition.
- **Create incentives for occupants and tenants.** Involve building occupants in energy efficiency strategies. Promote the use of energy-efficient computers and equipment, bill tenants from submeter readings to encourage energy conservation, educate occupants about shutting down computers and turning out lights before they leave, and give them regular feedback on energy performance.

Primary Resources: Cost-Effectiveness of Commissioning

Buildings are complex systems. Performance promised during planning and design can often by undermined by design flaws, construction defects, equipment malfunctions, and deferred maintenance. Building commissioning has emerged as an important quality-control strategy to detect and correct these deficiencies.

Commissioning is a systematic investigation of building performance with respect to performance goals, design specifications, and, most importantly, owner's requirements. Skilled engineers conduct a detailed study of building construction and performance. The cost of commissioning is often repaid with recovered energy performance. A recent Lawrence Berkeley National Laboratory study found that commissioning for existing buildings has a median cost of $0.27 per square foot and yields whole-building energy savings of 15%, with an average simple payback period of 0.7 years. For new construction, the median cost was determined to be $1 per square foot, with a median payback time of 4.8 years based on energy savings alone.

Overall, the Lawrence Berkeley study concluded that commissioning is one of the most cost-effective means of improving energy efficiency in commercial buildings.

- "Best Practices in Commissioning Existing Buildings" (Building Commissioning Association, 2008), http://www.bcxa.org/downloads/bca-ebcx-best-practices.pdf.
- "Commissioning for Great Buildings" (Building Commissioning Association, 2005), http://www.bcxa.org/downloads/bca-white-paper-cx.pdf.
- "Cost-Effectiveness of Commercial-Building Commissioning: Meta-Analysis of Energy and Non-Energy Impacts in Existing Buildings and New Construction," by Evan Mills (Lawrence Berkeley National Laboratory, 2004), http://eetd.lbl.gov/Emills/PUBS/Cx-Costs-Benefits.html.
- "The Value of the Commissioning Process: Costs and Benefits," by Chad Dorgan, Robert Cox, and Charles Dorgan (USGBC, 2002), http://www.usgbc.org/expo2002/schedule/documents/DS506_Dorgan_P152.pdf.

THINK ABOUT IT

Bridging the gap between design and operations. Engineers and architects often compare building performance with code requirements for new construction and speak of some percentage "better than code." Facility managers and building owners see invoices with dollars, kilowatts, therms, and gallons. This creates a gap between the metrics used to gauge building performance during design and operation. What are the consequences of this gap? What are the opportunities for closing it?

MATERIALS AND RESOURCES

Buildings generate a large amount of waste throughout their life cycles, from construction to building operations to demolition. The amount of waste leaving the property can be reduced, however, through responsible procurement choices, as well as by implementing comprehensive recycling programs throughout the construction, operation, and demolition phases. Consideration of materials and resources focuses on the health and productivity consequences of material selections for building occupants, plus the long-term social, economic, and environmental impacts of materials used in the design and construction of the building.

Green building addresses two kinds of problems related to materials and resources:

- Waste management; and
- Life-cycle impacts.

LEED recognizes and encourages strategies that consider materials and resources from a long-term, lifecycle perspective.

Assessments and Measurements

- **Rapidly renewable materials.** The amount of a building's agricultural products (fiber or animal) that are quickly grown or raised and can be harvested in a sustainable fashion, expressed as a percentage of the total materials cost. For LEED, rapidly renewable materials take 10 years or less to grow or raise.
- **Recycled content.** The percentage of material in a product that is recycled from the manufacturing waste stream (preconsumer waste) or the consumer waste stream (postconsumer waste) and used to make new materials. For LEED, recycled content is typically expressed as a percentage of the total material volume or weight.
- **Regional materials.** The amount of a building's materials that are extracted, processed, and manufactured close to a project site, expressed as a percentage of the total materials cost. For LEED, regional materials originate within 500 miles of the project site.
- **Reuse.** The amount of building materials returned to active use (in the same or a related capacity as their original use), expressed as a percentage of the total materials cost of a building. The salvaged materials are incorporated into the new building, thereby extending the lifetime of materials that would otherwise be discarded.
- **Sustainable forestry.** The practice of managing forest resources to meet the long-term forest product needs of humans while maintaining the biodiversity of forested landscapes.
- **Waste diversion.** The amount of waste disposed of other than through incineration or in landfills, expressed in tons. Examples of waste diversion include reuse and recycling.

THINK ABOUT IT

Materials matter. Which is more sustainable, a wood building or a steel building? Why?

WASTE MANAGEMENT

The intent of LEED credits in this category is to reduce the waste and toxins that are hauled to and disposed of in landfills or incineration facilities. During construction or renovation, materials should be recycled or reused whenever possible. During the daily operation of the building, recycling, reuse, and reduction programs can curb the amount of material destined for local landfills.

Strategies for reducing waste include the following:

- **Size the building appropriately.** Carefully match the size of the building to its intended function and owner's requirements. It may be possible to achieve the desired functions with a smaller building, thereby saving energy and reducing operating costs.
- **Develop a construction waste management policy.** Outline procedures and goals for construction waste diversion. This policy should specify a target diversion rate for the general contractor.

- **Encourage recycling.** Establish a waste reduction policy for operations and maintenance. Provide occupants with easily accessible collection bins for recyclables, and monitor the effectiveness of the policy.
- **Compost.** Institute an onsite composting program to turn landscaping debris into mulch.

Primary Resources: Waste Reduction

Solid waste is continually generated in most buildings as new products arrive and used materials leave as waste. This waste is transported to landfills or sometimes incinerated to generate energy. In either case, the disposal of solid waste produces greenhouse gas emissions. In landfills, a portion of the waste decays and produces methane—a potent greenhouse gas. Incineration of waste produces carbon dioxide as a byproduct. The result is that solid waste ultimately contributes directly to substantial greenhouse gas emissions.

The EPA has examined greenhouse gas emissions from building waste streams and estimates that the United States currently recycles approximately 32% of its solid waste—the carbon dioxide equivalent of removing almost 40 million cars from the road. The agency also estimates that improving recycling rates to just 35% could save more than 5 million metric tons of carbon dioxide equivalent. The construction and operation of green buildings can be an important part of achieving these reductions.

- Construction Materials Recycling Association, www.cdrecycling.org.
- Recycled Content Product Directory (California Integrated Waste Management Board), www.ciwmb.ca.gov/rcp.
- U.S. EPA information on the link between solid waste and greenhouse gas emissions, http://www.epa.gov/climatechange/wycd/waste/generalinfo.html.
- Waste Reduction Model (WARM) (U.S. EPA), www.epa.gov/warm.

THINK ABOUT IT

Embodied energy and emissions of solid waste. Many landfills burn the gas that seeps from buried piles of trash and garbage, and in some cases, this practice qualifies as a widely recognized method for creating "carbon offsets"—real, durable, verified reductions in greenhouse gas emissions. Why is burning landfill gas considered a reduction in greenhouse gas emissions? In other cases, landfill gas may be captured and used as fuel to generate electricity.

LIFE-CYCLE IMPACTS

LEED increasingly incorporates strategies intended to reduce the environmental impacts of materials acquired for construction, operation, maintenance, and upgrades of a building. To embed these strategies in the building's construction and operations processes, teams develop environmentally responsible procurement policies.

Strategies to promote sustainable purchasing during construction include the following:

- **Develop a construction purchasing policy.** Outline the goals, thresholds, and procedures for procurement of construction materials. Monitor compliance and track the effectiveness of the policy to ensure that it is working.
- **Specify green materials.** Rapidly renewable materials, regional materials, salvaged materials, and materials with recycled content reduce environmental impacts and promote sustainable material sources.
- **Specify green interiors.** Use finishes, carpets, fabric, and other materials with low levels of volatile organic compounds (VOCs), formaldehyde, and other potentially toxic chemicals to protect indoor environmental quality and reduce the life-cycle impacts of materials.

Strategies to promote sustainable purchasing during operations include these suggestions:

- **Develop a sustainable purchasing policy.** Outline the goals, thresholds, and procedures for procurement of ongoing consumables and durable goods. Monitor compliance to ensure that the policy is effective.
- **Specify green materials.** Give preference to rapidly renewable materials, regional materials, salvaged materials, and materials with recycled content.
- **Specify green electronic equipment.** Choose computers and appliances that meet ENERGY STAR, EPEAT (Electronic Product Environmental Assessment Tool), or other standards for efficient energy consumption.

THINK ABOUT IT

Sustainable product certification. Evaluating the sustainability of green products is complex, and competing claims make it difficult to determine the relative merits of many products. Third-party programs such as the Forest Stewardship Council and Green Seal offer independent measures of performance, but certifiers' varying and even conflicting standards can create confusion. What are the pros and cons of having different approaches to evaluating the sustainability of materials?

Primary Resources: Estimating Life-Cycle Impacts

Quantitative life-cycle assessment (LCA) involves an objective comparison of alternative design and construction practices. It relies on models and database-driven tools to analyze the environmental aspects and potential impacts associated with a product, process, or service. Several tools can help project teams conduct life-cycle assessments:

- **BEES 4.0 (Building for Environmental and Economic Sustainability).** This software tool helps balance the environmental and economic performance of building products. It is based on consensus standards and designed to be practical, flexible, consistent, and transparent. Visit http://www.wbdg.org/tools/bees.php.
- **Construction carbon calculator.** This Web-based tool helps developers, builders, architects, and land planners estimate the net embodied carbon of a project's structures and site. Visit http://buildcarbonneutral.org/.
- **ATHENA EcoCalculator for Assemblies.** This tool is used by architects, engineers, and other building professionals to characterize hundreds of design options based on databases, such as the U.S. Life-Cycle Inventory Database from the Department of Energy's National Renewable Energy Laboratory. Visit http://www.athenasmi.org/tools/docs/EcoCalculatorFactSheet.pdf.
- **EPEAT.** The Electronic Product Environmental Assessment Tool assists with the evaluation, comparison, and selection of computers and monitors based on their environmental attributes. See http://www.epeat.net/.

INDOOR ENVIRONMENTAL QUALITY

According to the EPA, Americans spend 90% of their time indoors, where concentrations of pollutants may be significantly higher than outdoor levels. Consequently, indoor environmental quality is a major concern in buildings.

Strategies to improve indoor environmental quality have the potential to enhance the lives of building occupants, increase the resale value of the building, and reduce liability for building owners. Personnel costs—primarily salaries and benefits—are much larger than the typical building's operating costs, such as electricity and maintenance. Thus, strategies that improve employee health and productivity over the long run can have a large return on investment. Moreover, preventing problems is generally much less expensive than dealing with any illnesses and loss of productivity stemming from poor indoor environmental quality. Building owners, designers, and operators should aim to provide stimulating and comfortable environments for the occupants and minimize the risk of building-related health problems. Meeting this goal requires attention to two kinds of issues:

- Indoor air quality; and
- Thermal comfort, lighting, and acoustics.

Assessments and Measurements

- **Carbon dioxide concentrations.** An indicator of ventilation effectiveness inside buildings. CO2 concentrations greater than 530 parts per million (ppm) above outdoor conditions generally indicate inadequate ventilation. Absolute concentrations of greater than 800 to 1,000 ppm generally indicate poor air quality for breathing. CO2 builds up in a space when there is not enough ventilation.
- **Controllability of systems.** The percentage of occupants who have direct control over temperature, airflow, and lighting in their spaces.
- **Minimum efficiency reporting value (MERV).** A rating that indicates the efficiency of air filters in the mechanical system. MERV ratings range from 1 (very low efficiency) to 16 (very high efficiency).
- **Thermal comfort.** The temperature, humidity, and airflow ranges within which the majority of people are most comfortable, as determined by ASHRAE Standard 55–2004. Because people dress differently depending on the season, thermal comfort levels vary with the season. Control setpoints for HVAC systems should vary accordingly, to ensure that occupants are comfortable and energy is conserved.
- **Ventilation rate.** The amount of air circulated through a space, measured in air changes per hour (the quantity of infiltration air in cubic feet per minute divided by the volume of the room). Proper ventilation rates, as prescribed by ASHRAE Standard 62, ensure that enough air is supplied for the number of occupants to prevent accumulation of carbon dioxide and other pollutants in the space.
- **Volatile organic compounds (VOCs).** The amount of carbon compounds that participate in atmospheric photochemical reactions and vaporize (become a gas) at normal room temperatures, measured in grams per liter. VOCs off-gas from many materials, including adhesives, sealants, paints, carpets, and particleboard. Limiting VOC concentrations protects the health of both construction personnel and building occupants.

THINK ABOUT IT

Biophilia. Humans evolved with a strong connection to nature. How can buildings reflect this connection? What are the benefits?

INDOOR AIR QUALITY

Protecting indoor environments from contaminants—such as volatile organic compounds (VOCs), carbon dioxide, particulates, and tobacco smoke—is essential to maintaining good indoor air quality. Off-gassing from furniture, carpets, paints, and cleaning products, plus human respiration, can create an indoor atmosphere that is hundreds of times more polluted than the outdoor environment. Ventilation is one effective way to control the concentration of pollutants indoors. New, low-emitting alternatives for interior finish materials are another; these products don't add pollutants to indoor environments and should be used in new building construction and renovations.

Strategies for maintaining indoor air quality include the following:

- **Prohibit smoking.** Institute a no-smoking policy in the building and around building entrances, operable windows, and air intakes.
- **Ensure adequate ventilation.** Appropriately size and operate ventilation systems to supply ample outside air to the occupants. Follow the most recent industry standards (such as ASHRAE Standard 62, Ventilation for Acceptable Indoor Air Quality).
- **Monitor carbon dioxide.** Install monitors and integrate them with a ventilation system that regulates the supply of air based on occupant demand. With demand-controlled ventilation, airflow is automatically increased if [carbon dioxide?] concentrations exceed a setpoint.
- **Install high-efficiency air filters.** Use filters with high MERV ratings in the ventilation equipment.
- **Specify low-emitting materials.** Use green materials for both new construction and renovations.
- **Protect air quality during construction.** Prevent mold by protecting all building materials from moisture exposure. Prevent dust and particulate buildup.
- **Conduct a flush-out.** Before occupancy, flush out indoor airborne contaminants by thoroughly exhausting old air and replacing it with outdoor air.
- **Employ a green cleaning program.** Select cleaning products and technologies to minimize the introduction of contaminants and the exposure of custodial staff.
- **Use integrated pest management.** A coordinated program of nonchemical strategies, such as monitoring and baiting, can reduce the use of pesticides and other potentially toxic contaminants.

THERMAL COMFORT, LIGHTING, AND ACOUSTICS

Thermal comfort, lighting, and acoustics are other major aspects of indoor environmental quality that have a significant impact on occupants. Access to daylight and views, a comfortable temperature, and good lighting and acoustic conditions can enhance occupants' sense of satisfaction in their space. These factors have been shown to improve human health and productivity. It has also been shown that occupants are more satisfied with their environment if they have control over these aspects. For example, the ability to open or close a window in their office allows workers to adapt to and tolerate temperatures outside the comfort zone in a sealed building environment.

Strategies for improving thermal comfort, lighting, and acoustics in indoor environments include these suggestions:

- **Use daylighting.** Design the building to provide ample access to natural daylight and views for the occupants. Service areas, equipment rooms, closets, and locker rooms should be located in the building core, with regularly occupied spaces placed around the perimeter of the building.
- **Install operable windows.** If possible, provide windows that can be opened to the outside.
- **Give occupants temperature control.** In mechanically ventilated buildings, provide thermostats that allow occupants to control the temperature in their immediate environment.
- **Give occupants ventilation control.** In mechanically ventilated buildings, provide adjustable air diffusers that allow occupants to adjust the airflow in their immediate environment.
- **Give occupants lighting control.** Provide occupants with adjustable lighting controls so that they can match the lighting levels to their tasks.
- **Conduct occupant surveys.** Use valid survey protocols to assess occupants' satisfaction with the indoor environment. Make operational changes based on the feedback.

THINK ABOUT IT

Thermal comfort. Experiments to determine thermal comfort norms for humans have been performed in carefully controlled laboratory environments where people were subjected to various environmental conditions. The standards developed through this research advised designers and operators to keep building environments within strictly defined ranges. However, recent research in real-world situations has shown that people are tolerant of more varied conditions when they have control over their environment. What are the energy efficiency implications of design that accommodate personal control over one's environment?

Primary Resources: Daylighting

A study of more than 2,000 California classrooms found that students in classrooms with the most daylight progressed 20% faster in math and 26% faster in reading than students in the classrooms with the least amount of natural light.

- "Daylight and Retail Sales" (California Energy Commission, 2003), http://www.h-m-g.com/downloads/Daylighting/A-5 Daylgt Retail 2.3.7.pdf.
- "Daylighting in Schools: An Investigation into the Relationship between Daylighting and Human Performance" (Heschong Mahone Group, 1999), http://h-m-g.com/projects/daylighting/summaries%20on%20daylighting.htm#Daylighting in Schools – PG&E 1999.
- "Healthier, Wealthier, Wiser: A Report on National Green Schools" (Global Green USA, no date), http://www.globalgreen.org/publications/.
- "Windows and Classrooms: A Study of Student Performance and the Indoor Environment" (California Energy Commission, 2003), http://www.h-m-g.com/downloads/Daylighting/A-7 Windows Classrooms 2.4.10.pdf.
- "Windows and Offices: A Study of Office Worker Performance and the Indoor Environment" (California Energy Commission, 2003), http://www.h-m-g.com/downloads/Daylighting/A-9 Windows Offices 2.6.10.pdf.

Indoor Environmental Quality

Studies by the Center for the Built Environment at the University of California–Berkeley have found that occupants of green buildings report significantly greater satisfaction with indoor air quality than occupants of conventional buildings. However, the benefits of green building don't extend to all aspects of indoor environmental quality. The green buildings often had superior air quality but provided less satisfaction in measures of acoustic quality.

- Indoor Environment Department, Lawrence Berkeley National Laboratory, http://eetd.lbl.gov/ied/ied.html.
- Information on indoor health and productivity, http://www.ihpcentral.org.
- "Occupant Satisfaction with Indoor Environmental Quality in Green Buildings" (Center for the Built Environment, 2006), http://www.cbe.berkeley.edu/research/pdf files/Abbaszadeh HB2006.pdf.

INNOVATION IN DESIGN

The LEED rating systems offer Innovation in Design credits to encourage projects to go above and beyond the credit requirements and explore innovative green building strategies. LEED recognizes two strategies for earning Innovation in Design credits: exceptional performance and innovation.

Exemplary performance strategies surpass the requirements of existing LEED credits and substantially exceed the performance-based standards for energy, water, or waste management. LEED has recognized the following kinds of exemplary performance:

- Doubling density requirements for Sustainable Sites credits;
- Significantly reducing indoor water use beyond the LEED requirement of 40%;
- Significantly diverting construction waste beyond the requirement of 75%; and
- Providing more daylighting than the 75% requirement.

Innovative strategies expand the breadth of green building practice and introduce new ideas, such as these recent innovative strategies:

- Developing an educational outreach program;
- Using a greenhouse gas budget to demonstrate carbon-neutral design and operations; and
- Incorporating high levels of fly ash in concrete to divert waste material from landfills.

Strategies and practices rewarded as innovative today may become credits in the future. In fact, as LEED continues to evolve and today's innovation becomes tomorrow's standard, strategies that may have earned an Innovation in Design credit in the past may not necessarily earn recognition in current or future projects.

Primary Resource: Guidance on Innovation in Design Credits

Requirements for documenting the achievement of Innovation in Design credits are available from USGBC, at http://www.usgbc.org/Docs/LEEDdocs/IDcredit_guidance_final.pdf.

Project Case Study

©The Kubala Washatko Architects, Inc./Mark F. Heffron

The Aldo Leopold Legacy Center

The Aldo Leopold Legacy Center was the first building recognized by USGBC as carbon neutral—an exceptional achievement that earned the center an Innovation in Design credit. The project team prepared a greenhouse gas emissions budget based on the requirements of the World Resources Institute Greenhouse Gas Protocol. Conservatively accounting for carbon generation and sequestration in metric tons of CO_2 equivalent (a measure of greenhouse gas emissions that combines multiple heat-trapping gases, such carbon dioxide, methane, and nitrous oxide), the activities of the center will result in the net *reduction* of CO_2 emissions each year.

Projected Annual Greenhouse Gas Emissions From Aldo Leopold Legacy Center

	CO_2 Equivalent per Year (Metric Tons)	
Total emissions		13.42
Offset from renewable energy	–6.24	
Onsite forest sequestration	–8.75	
Total emissions reduction		–14.99
Net balance of emissions		–1.57

More information about the Aldo Leopold Legacy Center is available at http://www.aldoleopold.org/legacycenter/carbonneutral.html.

GLOSSARY

acid rain the precipitation of dilute solutions of strong mineral acids, formed by the mixing in the atmosphere of various industrial pollutants (primarily sulfur dioxide and nitrogen oxides) with naturally occurring oxygen and water vapor.

adapted plants nonnative, introduced plants that reliably grow well in a given habitat with minimal winter protection, pest control, fertilization, or irrigation once their root systems are established. Adapted plants are considered low maintenance and not invasive.

air quality standards the level of pollutants prescribed by regulations that is not to be exceeded during a given time in a defined area. (EPA)

alternative fuel vehicles vehicles that use low-polluting, nongasoline fuels, such as electricity, hydrogen, propane or compressed natural gas, liquid natural gas, methanol, and ethanol. In LEED, efficient gas-electric hybrid vehicles are included in this group.

ambient temperature the temperature of the surrounding air or other medium. (EPA)

ASHRAE American Society of Heating, Refrigerating and Air-Conditioning Engineers.

bake-out a process used to remove volatile organic compounds (VOCs) from a building by elevating the temperature in the fully furnished and ventilated building prior to human occupancy.

biodegradable capable of decomposing under natural conditions. (EPA)

biodiversity the variety of life in all forms, levels, and combinations, including ecosystem diversity, species diversity, and genetic diversity.

biomass plant material from trees, grasses, or crops that can be converted to heat energy to produce electricity.

bioswale a stormwater control feature that uses a combination of an engineered basin, soils, and vegetation to slow and detain stormwater, increase groundwater recharge, and reduce peak stormwater runoff.

blackwater wastewater from toilets and urinals; definitions vary, and wastewater from kitchen sinks (perhaps differentiated by the use of a garbage disposal), showers, or bathtubs is considered blackwater under some state or local codes.

British thermal unit (Btu) the amount of heat required to raise the temperature of one pound of liquid water from 60° to 61° Fahrenheit. This standard measure of energy is used to describe the energy content of fuels and compare energy use.

brownfield real property whose use may be complicated by the presence or possible presence of a hazardous substance, pollutant, or contaminant.

building density the floor area of the building divided by the total area of the site (square feet per acre).

building envelope the exterior surface of a building—the walls, windows, roof, and floor; also referred to as the building shell.

building footprint the area on a project site that is used by the building structure, defined by the perimeter of the building plan. Parking lots, landscapes, and other nonbuilding facilities are not included in the building footprint.

byproduct material, other than the principal product, generated as a consequence of an industrial process or as a breakdown product in a living system. (EPA)

carbon footprint a measure of greenhouse gas emissions associated with an activity. A comprehensive carbon footprint includes building construction, operation, energy use, building-related transportation, and the embodied energy of water, solid waste, and construction materials.

chiller a device that removes heat from a liquid, typically as part of a refrigeration system used to cool and dehumidify buildings.

commissioning (Cx) the process of verifying and documenting that a building and all of its systems and assemblies are planned, designed, installed, tested, operated, and maintained to meet the owner's project requirements.

commissioning plan a document that outlines the organization, schedule, allocation of resources, and documentation requirements of the commissioning process.

commissioning report a document that details the commissioning process, including a commissioning program overview, identification of the commissioning team, and description of the commissioning process activities.

compact fluorescent lamp (CFL) a small fluorescent lamp, used as a more efficient alternative to incandescent lighting; also called a PL, twin-tube, or biax lamp. (EPA)

construction and demolition debris waste and recyclables generated from construction and from the renovation, demolition, or deconstruction of existing structures. It does not include land-clearing debris, such as soil, vegetation, and rocks.

construction waste management plan a plan that diverts construction debris from landfills through recycling, salvaging, and reuse.

contaminant an unwanted airborne element that may reduce indoor air quality (ASHRAE Standard 62.1–2007).

cooling tower a structure that uses water to absorb heat from air-conditioning systems and regulate air temperature in a facility.

daylighting the controlled admission of natural light into a space, used to reduce or eliminate electric lighting.

dry ponds excavated areas that detain stormwater and slow runoff but are dry between rain events. Wet ponds serve a similar function but are designed to hold water all the time.

ecosystem a basic unit of nature that includes a community of organisms and their nonliving environment linked by biological, chemical and physical processes.

energy-efficient products and systems building components and appliances that use less energy to perform as well as or better than standard products.

energy management system a control system capable of monitoring environmental and system loads and adjusting HVAC operations accordingly in order to conserve energy while maintaining comfort. (EPA)

ENERGY STAR® rating a measure of a building's energy performance compared with that of similar buildings, as determined by the ENERGY STAR Portfolio Manager. A score of 50 represents average building performance.

environmental sustainability long-term maintenance of ecosystem components and functions for future generations. (EPA)

flush-out the operation of mechanical systems for a minimum of two weeks using 100 percent outside air at the end of construction and prior to building occupancy to ensure safe indoor air quality.

fossil fuel energy derived from ancient organic remains, such as peat, coal, crude oil, and natural gas. (EPA)

graywater domestic wastewater composed of wash water from kitchen, bathroom, and laundry sinks, tubs, and washers. (EPA) The Uniform Plumbing Code (UPC) defines graywater in its Appendix G, "Gray Water Systems for Single-Family Dwellings", as "untreated household waste water which has not come into contact with toilet waste. Gray water includes used water from bathtubs, showers, bathroom wash basins, and water from clothes-washer and laundry tubs. It must not include waste water from kitchen sinks or dishwashers." The International Plumbing Code (IPC) defines graywater in its Appendix C, Gray Water Recycling Systems, as "waste water discharged from lavatories, bathtubs, showers, clothes washers and laundry sinks." Some states and local authorities allow kitchen sink wastewater to be included in graywater. Other differences with the UPC and IPC definitions can likely be found in state and local codes. Project teams should comply with graywater definitions as established by the authority having jurisdiction in the project area.

harvested rainwater precipitation captured and used for indoor needs, irrigation, or both.

heat island effect the absorption of heat by hardscapes, such as dark, nonreflective pavement and buildings, and its radiation to surrounding areas. Particularly in urban areas, other sources may include vehicle exhaust, air-conditioners, and street equipment; reduced airflow from tall buildings and narrow streets exacerbates the effect.

high-performance green building a structure designed to conserve water and energy; use space, materials, and resources efficiently; minimize construction waste; and create a healthful indoor environment.

HVAC systems equipment, distribution systems, and terminals that provide the processes of heating, ventilating, or air-conditioning. (ASHRAE Standard 90.1–2007)

indoor air quality the nature of air inside the space that affects the health and well-being of building occupants. It is considered acceptable when there are no known contaminants at harmful concentrations and a substantial majority (80% or more) of the occupants do not express dissatisfaction. (ASHRAE Standard 62.1–2007)

integrated design team all the individuals involved in a building project from early in the design process, including the design professionals, the owner's representatives, and the general contractor and subcontractors.

LEED credit an optional LEED Green Building Rating System™ component whose achievement results in the earning of points toward certification.

LEED Credit Interpretation Request a formal USGBC process in which a project team experiencing difficulties in the application of a LEED prerequisite or credit can seek and receive clarification, issued as a **Credit Interpretation Ruling.** Typically, difficulties arise when specific issues are not directly addressed by LEED reference guides or a conflict between credit requirements arises.

LEED® Green Building Rating System™ a voluntary, consensus-based, market-driven building rating system based on existing, proven technology. The LEED Green Building Rating System™ represents USGBC's effort to provide a national benchmark for green buildings. Through its use as a design guideline and third-party certification tool, the LEED Green Building Rating

System aims to improve occupant well-being, environmental performance, and economic returns using established and innovative practices, standards, and technologies. as a design guideline and third-party certification tool, the LEED Green Building Rating System™ aims to improve occupant well-being, environmental performance, and economic returns using established and innovative practices, standards, and technologies.

LEED intent the primary goal of each prerequisite or credit.

LEED prerequisite a required LEED Green Building Rating System™ component whose achievement is mandatory and does not earn any points.

LEED technical advisory group (TAG) a committee consisting of industry experts who assist in interpreting credits and developing technical improvements to the LEED Green Building Rating System™.

life-cycle assessment an analysis of the environmental aspects and potential impacts associated with a product, process, or service.

market transformation systematic improvements in the performance of a market or market segment. For example, EPA's ENERGY STAR program has shifted the performance of homes, buildings, and appliances toward higher levels of energy efficiency by providing recognition and comparative performance information through its ENERGY STAR labels.

native (or indigenous) plants plants adapted to a given area during a defined time period. In North America, the term often refers to plants growing in a region prior to the time of settlement by people of European descent. Native plants are considered low maintenance and not invasive.

nonpotable water. See **potable water.**

nonrenewable not capable of being replaced; permanently depleted once used. Examples of nonrenewable energy sources are oil and natural gas; nonrenewable natural resources include metallic ores.

off-gassing the emission of volatile organic compounds from synthetic and natural products.

particulates solid particles or liquid droplets in the atmosphere. The chemical composition of particulates varies, depending on location and time of year. Sources include dust, emissions from industrial processes, combustion products from the burning of wood and coal, combustion products associated with motor vehicle or nonroad engine exhausts, and reactions to gases in the atmosphere. (EPA)

perviousness the percentage of the surface area of a paving material that is open and allows moisture to pass through the material and soak into the ground below.

photovoltaic (PV) energy electricity from photovoltaic cells that convert the energy in sunlight into electricity.

pollutant any substance introduced into the environment that harms the usefulness of a resource or the health of humans, animals, or ecosystems. (EPA) Air pollutants include emissions of carbon dioxide (CO_2), sulfur dioxide (SO_2), nitrogen oxides (NO_x), mercury (Hg), small particulates (PM2.5), and large particulates (PM10).

postconsumer recycled content the percentage of material in a product that was consumer waste. The recycled material was generated by household, commercial, industrial, or institutional end users and can no longer be used for its intended purpose. This includes returns of materials from the distribution chain. Examples include construction and demolition debris, materials collected through recycling programs, discarded products (such as furniture, cabinetry, and decking), and landscaping waste (such as leaves, grass clippings, and tree trimmings). (ISO 14021)

potable water water that meets or exceeds the EPA's drinking water quality standards and is approved for human consumption by the state or local authorities having jurisdiction; it may be supplied from wells or municipal water systems.

preconsumer recycled content the percentage of material in a product that was recycled from manufacturing waste. Preconsumer content was formerly known as postindustrial content. Examples include planer shavings, sawdust, bagasse, walnut shells, culls, trimmed materials, overissue publications, and obsolete inventories. Excluded are rework, regrind, or scrap materials capable of being reclaimed within the same process that generated them. (ISO 14021)

rain garden a stormwater management feature consisting of an excavated depression and vegetation that collects and filters runoff and reduce peak discharge rates.

rainwater harvesting the collection and storage of precipitation from a catchment area, such as a roof.

rapidly renewable materials agricultural products, both fiber and animal, that take 10 years or less to grow or raise and can be harvested in a sustainable fashion.

regenerative design sustainable plans for built environments that improve existing conditions. Regenerative design goes beyond reducing impacts to create positive change in the local and global environments.

renewable energy resources that are not depleted by use. Examples include energy from the sun, wind, and small (low-impact) hydropower, plus geothermal energy and wave and tidal systems. Ways to capture energy from the sun include photovoltaic, solar thermal, and bioenergy systems based on wood waste, agricultural crops or residue, animal and other organic waste, or landfill gas.

renewable energy certificate (REC) a tradable commodity representing proof that a unit of electricity was generated from a renewable energy resource. RECs are sold separately from the electricity itself and thus allow the purchase of green power by a user of conventionally generated electricity.

salvaged material construction items recovered from existing buildings or construction sites and reused. Common salvaged materials include structural beams and posts, flooring, doors, cabinetry, brick, and decorative items.

sick building syndrome (SBS) a combination of symptoms, experienced by occupants of a building, that appear to be linked to time spent in the building but cannot be traced to a specific cause. Complaints may be localized in a particular room or zone or be spread throughout the building. (EPA)

stormwater runoff water from precipitation that flows over surfaces into sewer systems or receiving water bodies. All precipitation that leaves project site boundaries on the surface is considered stormwater runoff.

sustainability meeting the needs of the present without compromising the ability of future generations to meet their own needs. (Brundtland Commission)

sustainable forestry management of forest resources to meet the long-term forest product needs of humans while maintaining the biodiversity of forested landscapes. The primary goal is to restore, enhance, and sustain a full range of forest values, including economic, social, and ecological considerations.

sustained-yield forestry management of a forest to produce in perpetuity a high-level annual or regular periodic output, through a balance between increment and cutting. (Society of American Foresters)

thermal comfort the condition that exists when occupants express satisfaction with the thermal environment.

volatile organic compound (VOC) a carbon compound that participates in atmospheric photochemical reactions (excluding carbon monoxide, carbon dioxide, carbonic acid, metallic carbides and carbonates, and ammonium carbonate). Such compounds vaporize (become a gas) at normal room temperatures.

wastewater the spent or used water from a home, community, farm, or industry that contains dissolved or suspended matter. (EPA)

wetland vegetation plants that require saturated soils to survive or can tolerate prolonged wet soil conditions.

xeriscaping a landscaping method that makes routine irrigation unnecessary by using drought-adaptable and low-water plants, as well as soil amendments such as compost and mulches to reduce evaporation.